Love and peace
Cynthia Stotlar
and
Tammy S Patterson

A Caregiver's Companion

Spiritual Support for the Stressed-Out Soul

CYNTHIA B. STOTLAR

CROSSBOOKS
PUBLISHING

CrossBooks™
A Division of LifeWay
1663 Liberty Drive
Bloomington, IN 47403
www.crossbooks.com
Phone: 1-866-879-0502

Cover photo and design by Tammy Patterson, TSCPgraphics at www.tscpgraphics.com

First published by CrossBooks 2/7/2012

ISBN: 978-1-4627-1287-8 (hc)
ISBN: 978-1-4627-1288-5 (sc)
ISBN: 978-1-4627-1289-2 (e)

Library of Congress Control Number: 2011963047

Printed in the United States of America

This book is printed on acid-free paper.

Any people depicted in stock imagery provided by Thinkstock are models, and such images are being used for illustrative purposes only.

Certain stock imagery © Thinkstock.

Contents

Dedication

Many people offered me amazing support during the journey through Dave's illness. This book is dedicated to all of them. Dr. Caricioni and Jennifer Nelson at Stormont Vail's Cancer Center in Topeka, Kansas, were both wonderfully kind and gracious caregivers. They always lent an ear and an understanding heart as well as great medical advice. The folks at both Midland Hospice in Topeka, Kansas, and Seasons Hospice in Chicago, Illinois, offered amazing support during the difficult and tumultuous time.

We must also thank all the neighbors, friends, and family without whom we both would have collapsed under the stress. Many thanks to our bridge group wives: Paula Ackerman, Pam Boetcher, Judy Wunder, Sue Hein, Amy McLaren, Marj Nelson, and Karen Kluczykowski. These women delivered many wonderful meals. Many thanks to my Sunday-school group at Topeka Bible Church, who prayed hard for Dave and me and who also rallied to the meal calls when asked. Thanks to friends across the miles who stayed in touch and worked to keep me laughing: Cinda Moss, May Bennett, Betty Dlouhy, Dorothy Essex, Beth O'Leary, Ruth and Joe Lokey, Pat Flynn, and Tom Fiddelke.

A huge thanks must go to our employees: Alisa Mezger-Crawford, Amanda Brown, Ann Stephens, Debbie Ramberg, Jeremy Hall, and John and Kristina Dietrick. They kept the business running, and running well, when neither Dave nor I was able.

Our children and their spouses were beyond supportive. During Dave's final weeks, Jason, our youngest, came to Topeka to meet with doctors. He sat down with his dad and discussed Dave's mortality and my inability to care for him alone; then he helped me bring Dave up to Chicago. Eric, our eldest, and his wife, Kimberly, opened their home to us. They threw their lives into disarray to welcome and support us as we made the hospice journey together. Once there, Eric, Kimberly, Jason, and his wife, Julia, did everything in their power to make the situation as positive as possible.

Finally, a huge thanks goes to the best neighbor and friend a person could be blessed to have, Debbie Whelan. Without her, I would have been lost. Thanks to the unfailing support of her husband, Ward, and my other neighbors and dear friends Doug Eby, Stephanie and Jeremy Hall, Mike Warren, and Amy and Greg McLaren, my yard and house did not fall into disrepair, and I was able to keep my head above water.

My office help consists of JoJo, Jimmi and Gracie
– a perfect trifecta of emotional support.

Introduction

I've seen cancer from both sides now, as Joni Mitchell sang. Like her, I don't begin to think I know all there is about cancer or being a caregiver. I do want to help others who are walking that same path, though.

In 1996, I was diagnosed with stage II aggressive breast cancer, and I spent the next year in treatment. When people expressed sympathy, I'd often tell them I thought it was harder on my husband, David, than it was on me. And I really meant it. Yes, I was ill, I felt lousy, and I lost my hair; but it was perfectly acceptable for me to have a meltdown, cry, rant, be cranky, or be depressed. His role as supportive spouse was much more challenging. David was not supposed to get grumpy, irritable, or depressed. He was supposed to be optimistic, calm, rational, and, well, supportive. My wish was his command, even if that wish meant he had to get something I wanted after he'd had a very hard day at work. He was amazing at it! Plus, he did it without much support from family or friends. Our family was hundreds of miles away, he chose not to tell anyone at his office, and he had very few close friends with whom to share his burden. He internalized his stress.

In February 2008, David was diagnosed with an extremely aggressive stage IV colon cancer, and he was given one to six months to live. This was the day before our twenty-fifth wedding anniversary. He was checked into the hospital that night to get a port installed for the chemotherapy and have more tests run. The tables turned; now it was *my* turn to be the supportive spouse. I realized I was not nearly as good at it as he had been! We joked several times afterwards that we both wished it had been me diagnosed with cancer, as I was much better at being sick, and he was much better at playing nurse. For example, David was our primary cook (yes, I am one of the lucky few women who married a man who loved to cook). He quickly lost the energy to cook, and we were in trouble when it came to food preparation.

David was called home to heaven on August 19, 2008. I worked on ways to calm my stress and come at the situation from the spiritual perspective Job displayed when he said, "The Lord gave and the Lord has taken away, may the name of the Lord be praised" (Job 1:21). My belief system states that illness does not come from God as a punishment or test of faith. It is simply a fact of the human condition: no one gets out alive. But faith in God and His faith in us help us through illnesses and other life struggles.

I realized the catastrophe of my husband's death was not just happening to me. As we baby boomers age, it will become more and more common. For whatever reason, we women tend to outlive the men, and it is often the women who find themselves the stressed-out caregivers in need of spiritual support.

Having taught stress-management classes to business professionals for more than thirty years, I decided to meld that knowledge with spiritual teachings and write *The Caregiver's Companion*, a blend of stress-management techniques and spiritual reflections to help others through the same journey I took. Just in my immediate circle of friends, I have one friend whose husband died of a massive heart attack at the young age of thirty-eight, while another woman's husband died after a six-week battle with cancer. A neighbor lost her husband to cancer in only two short months, and another dear friend's husband recently died from kidney cancer.

At church, we went through a series of teachings entitled *Next Steps*. The three key concepts of this series were:

1. Spend more time with Christ and dig deeper into His Word.
2. Care and mentor others.
3. Reach out to the world with your ministry to others.

Our pastor, Jim Congdon, preached from Matthew 28:16-20 about the sweeping claim that Jesus has total authority over all heaven and Earth. Jesus frees us from guilt, pain, and suffering, and he commands us to go and make disciples. Each of us has a calling we should follow; we all have a gift to share. We have the confidence that Jesus is always with us. There is no downside to believing in Christ. At church, we were challenged to find our next step. It could be making a prayer commitment, making a change commitment, or doing a mission trip. At that service, I decided this book represented my next step. I also set up a meeting with Patty Diliberto, the women's ministry leader, to set things in motion for an outreach to stressed-out spouses.

In Matthew 28:16-20, we read, "Jesus had told them to go. When they saw him, they worshiped him; but some doubted. Then Jesus came to them and said, 'All authority in heaven and on earth has been given to me. Therefore go and make disciples of all nations, baptizing them in the name of the Father and of the Son and of the Holy Spirit, and teaching them to obey everything I have commanded you and surely I am with you always, to the very end of the age.'" My hope for each of you reading this is that it offers some glimmers of hope or a semblance of support and guidance from God. I firmly believe God has a plan for each of us. The challenge is slowing down long enough to listen to Him as He answers our many prayers for guidance. I hear Him telling me this is my calling at this time. I believe the way for me to find my own spiritual support is to help others find theirs.

There is a Latin proverb that says, "By learning you will teach; by teaching you will learn." Elisabeth Kubler-Ross, psychiatrist and author of *On Death and Dying*, wrote, "All events are blessings given to us to learn from." There are numerous tips and techniques in this book. You are not expected to try them all. Instead, read through them and select those that could easily add to your life and bring you joy or relief. Try them. Reread the book periodically, and select others at different times. If your loved one is seriously ill over a number of years, you will need to keep varying the techniques used to help cope with the stress of being a constant caregiver.

Proverbs 24:14
Know also that wisdom is sweet to your soul, if you find it, there is a future hope for you, and your hope will not be cut off.

Romans 8:26–27
In the same way, the Spirit helps us in our weakness. We do not know what we ought to pray for, but the Spirit himself intercedes for us with groans that words cannot express. And he who searches our hearts knows the mind of the Spirit, because the Spirit intercedes for the saints in accordance with God's will.

Disclaimer

Just because you work through these exercises and use the stress tips inside does not mean you will never have a meltdown, cry, or be depressed. You will. It is a normal, natural thing to do. In fact, I'd be more surprised if you didn't have those reactions. But if you work consciously to reduce your stress during this very trying period of your life, you will develop skills that will serve you well forever.

I know I have cried my heart out over losing Dave. For me, I lost a loving husband and a brilliant business partner. He had a very philosophical, scholarly, and intelligent mind, but he was also a fun-loving friend and an adventurous travel buddy. My solace comes from knowing he is in heaven now having great philosophical conversations with the likes of Einstein and Asimov.

Chapters 12 and 13 are for those of you providing caregiving to terminally ill loved ones. Many of you are blessed enough not to be in that situation, and you won't need these final two chapters.

Set your pace...Focus

1. Meditation and Prayer

James 5:16
Therefore confess your sins to each other and pray
for each other so that you may be healed. The prayer
of a righteous man is powerful and effective.

Take time to be alone with God.

Prayer and Meditation

Meditation has been shown to alter brain waves and reduce stress. Prayer is a form of meditation. Turning over your worries or problems to a higher power can be freeing. Practicing either meditation or prayer on a daily basis can be an excellent stress-reduction and prevention technique.[1]

Prayer is especially beneficial by developing our trust and reliance on God, bringing a sense of peace and direction; our ability to seek God's direction, diminishing the burden of trying to cope on our own strength; our ability to focus on God so we feel less alone; and our ability to focus on God's love and faithfulness, which helps us develop a perspective on our tribulations and helps us see God in the midst of our troubles.

Prayer Practices

You may wish to pray in a set manner or learn a new way. The ACTS method is based on the Lord's Prayer. Each letter signifies a different section of the prayer.[2] The ACTS approach is taught in many churches, and it goes as follows:

- **A** is for *adoration* of God. There are many reasons to express your adoration of God. Just follow what the Bible tells you, and reasons to love God will be plentiful.
- **C** is for *confession* of your sins and shortcomings. In this case, "sin" is a broad term, encompassing everything from breaking commandments to slacking on personal morals and ideals. For example, maybe you don't visit your loved ones as much as you believe you should, or you get angry with them over something little.
- **T** is for giving *thanks* for your blessings. Give thanks for all the world has to offer. Think about all that God has blessed you with. Thank Him for the wonderful memories you have and the time you and your loved one spent together. I realize caregivers face daily trials and tribulations, and being thankful is often challenging when everything around you seems to be imploding. I understand there will be days when you won't feel very thankful or much adoration for God. However, try looking for the good. It can really help you turn your focus away from the negatives, which are so very easy to see. When I had cancer, I kept a gratitude journal and forced myself to find at least one good thing about each day. Amazingly, even on chemo days when the meds made me ill, there would still be something positive. Maybe it was a caring nurse, a card someone sent, or my loving hubby that cheered me up. Try it. You might just like it.

- **S** is for *supplication* and requesting God's support. You can seek support for anything: financial help, relationship help, health guidance, and more.

Another technique is the Five Finger Prayer. A friend shared this with me, and I have been using it.

1. Your thumb is nearest you, so begin your prayers by praying for those closest to you. They are the easiest to remember. To pray for our loved ones is, as C. S. Lewis once said, a "sweet duty."
2. The next finger is the pointing finger. Pray for those who teach, instruct, and heal. This includes teachers, doctors, and ministers. They need support and wisdom in pointing others in the right direction. Keep them in your prayers.
3. The next finger is the tallest finger. It reminds us of our leaders. Pray for the president, leaders in business and industry, and administrators. These people shape our nation and guide public opinion. They need God's guidance, especially in our turbulent times.
4. The fourth finger is our ring finger. Surprisingly to many, the ring finger is our weakest finger, as any piano teacher will testify. It should remind us to pray for those who are weak, in trouble, or in pain. They need your prayers day and night. You cannot pray too much for them.
5. Lastly comes our pinkie finger. It is the smallest finger of all, which is where we should place ourselves in relation to God and others. As the Bible says, "The least shall be the greatest among you." Your pinkie should remind you to pray for yourself. By the time you have prayed for the other four groups, your own needs will be put into proper perspective, and you will be able to pray for yourself more effectively.

You may wish to find a particular passage of scripture to study at length. Many in my Sunday school class have enjoyed reading the Psalms. The book of Job is often comforting as well since he had much to overcome yet never lost his faith.

The Twenty-third Psalm, with which you may already be familiar, can be helpful during your time as a caregiver. You may feel alone while you act as shepherd for your loved one. Never forget, though, even when it feels you are taking care of everything, God is taking care of you.

The Lord is my shepherd; I shall not be in want.
He makes me lie down in green pastures,
He leads me beside quiet waters.
He restores my soul.
He guides me in paths of righteousness
for his name's sake.
Even though I walk in the valley of the shadow of
death, I will fear no evil, for you are with me;
Your rod and your staff, they comfort me.
You prepare a table before me in
the presence of my enemies.
You anointest my head with oil; my cup overflows.
Surely goodness and love will follow me
all the days of my life, and I will dwell
in the house of the Lord forever.

Forgiveness Figures In

Practicing regular forgiveness is very freeing. Often the person with whom you are angry does not even know that you feel wronged. Holding onto anger can hurt your body. By forgiving the person and the offense, you release the anger.[3]

Every evening after your prayers, ask the Lord to forgive anyone you feel wronged you that day. Then ask that the Lord bless that person too. Also, every day before you leave work, ask God to forgive anyone who irritated you that day and ask that they be blessed on their way home. Perhaps your coworker took an extra doughnut and you didn't get one at all, or your boss took the last of the coffee and didn't make a new pot, or your direct report didn't get some data to you in a timely manner—whatever the wrong, you, and God, can forgive it. You'll be surprised how much better you feel knowing you have not only let go of the irritation but also asked for that person to be blessed. Try it for a week. You'll find it comforting.

According to an article on WebMD,[4] researchers at Hope College in Holland, Michigan, say forgiveness seems to be better for people than holding a grudge, at least in terms of negative effects on the body. Forgiveness is something nearly all Americans believe in but don't always practice. In a recent nationwide Gallup poll, 94 percent of respondents said it was important to forgive, while only 48 percent said they usually tried to forgive others. Philosopher Friedrich Nietzsche once equated forgiveness with weakness. But Charlotte van Oyen Witvliet, PhD, the lead researcher in the study, believes that failure to forgive can weaken a person's health.

Here is a handy chart you can use as a jumping-off point for forgiving those who trespass against you. Think through the last week. Did someone take the last soda from the work fridge? Did someone cut in front of you in the checkout lane? These people can be forgiven too. Why be mad at them any longer?

Person to Forgive	Reason They Need Forgiveness	Blessing You Wish for Them
Person in "10 Items or Less" checkout lane has 20 items.	Being in a hurry and being selfish.	That they get where they need to go in the right amount of time safely and with a sense of peace.

Neal T. Anderson's *The Bondage Breaker* gives this wonderful sample prayer. "Lord, I choose to forgive (name) for (offense). I choose to no longer hold this against (name), and I ask you to bless (name). Thank you for setting me free from the bondage of unforgiveness."

You may need to forgive your loved one for some past grievances as well. Do not be surprised if you are angry your loved one is dying and leaving you on your own. Anger is a very normal and natural reaction. It stems from the fear of being left alone.

It is important to determine whether the cause of your anger is fear or something that truly needs forgiveness. This will be easier said than done. You should start working on this before too much time passes. You may wish to verbally tell your loved one you forgive him or her for whatever is bothering you before he or she passes.

Here is another handy chart you can use as a jumping-off point for thinking though how to actually *show* you have forgiven someone.

Things to Forgive Your Loved One For Doing	How Can you Show Your Forgiveness?
Example: Made a bad decision on investments that cost serious money.	*Give him/her a card stating your forgiveness then don't bring it up again (and again).*

Colossians 3:13
Bear with each other and forgive whatever
grievances you may have against one another.
Forgive as the Lord forgave you.

Ephesians 4:32
Be kind and compassionate to one another,
forgiving each other, just as in
Christ God forgave you.

You may also need to work on forgiving God. After all, He has decided to take someone you love away from you, for some unfathomable reason. I read and reread the book of Job during Dave's illness. God allowed bad things to happen to Job as a test of his faithfulness, but because he passed the test, good things once again began to happen. I've meditated on this concept, and I know that without Dave's illness, I would not have set out on the journey to write this book or reach out to others in this situation.

I attended the funeral of a friend who passed away from cancer at the age of fifty-eight. He had lived an amazingly full and spiritual life. One of the focuses of his funeral was that he had been a gift from God to his family and the community. We were encouraged to focus on the good times we had, to be grateful God had shared his spirit with us in the first place, and not to be angry he was back with God. The pastor reviewed his amazing accomplishments, showing fun pictures along with the stories. Family members, friends, and business associates all shared their tales of how he had touched their lives for the better. We all left the service knowing he had accomplished a tremendous amount of God's work in his relatively short time on Earth. The hard part came later. It is tough not dwelling on what you lost, but instead focusing on what you gained.

Mother Teresa was remarkable for her unselfishness. As a caregiver, you may feel similar to Mother Theresa in that your free time is suddenly and drastically reduced. I love her poem below. Depending on the day, a different verse applies best. As a caregiver, the line "The good you do today may be forgotten tomorrow." will ring very true. It often seems a thankless job. But your Father in heaven is watching, and your loved one knows the difference. That is all that really matters.

People are often unreasonable and self-centered.
Forgive then anyway.
If you are kind, people may accuse
you of ulterior motives.
Be kind anyway.
If you are honest, people may cheat you.
Be honest anyway.
If you find happiness, people may be jealous.
Be happy anyway.
The good you do today may be forgotten tomorrow.
Do good anyway.
Give the world the best you have,
and it may never be enough.
Give your best anyway.
For you see, in the end, it is between you and God.
It was never between you and them anyway.
—Mother Teresa

Chapter One Worksheet: Mediation and Prayer

What was the most powerful thought or strongest concept in this chapter for you?

_____

_____

_____

_____

If you were to implement one idea from this chapter, what would it be?

_____

_____

_____

_____

What do you plan to do differently as a result of what you read in this chapter?

_____

_____

_____

_____

Which concept(s) would you like to share with family or friends?

_____

_____

_____

_____

Allow God's love to give you comfort and peace.

2. Stress Buster Basics

Soar to new heights...

Focus on doing
what you do well
and find joy in the moment.

Sleep Soothes the Soul

Many Americans are chronically sleep-deprived. Frequently, they get six hours of sleep or less each night.[1] Sleep-deprivation makes you tired, irritable, and fuzzy-headed—none of which makes caring for a loved one any easier. As difficult as it might be, try to get at least eight hours of sleep a night to help reduce your stress level and give you more energy to deal with the added stress of depression and grief.[2] One of the top stresses of a caregiver is exhaustion, but getting the necessary amount of sleep can help ease this stressor.[3]

> *Proverbs 3:24*
> *When you lie down, you will not be afraid;*
> *when you lie down, your sleep will be sweet.*

Evenings in Earnest

Get yourself organized at night for less stress in the morning. For example, lay out your clothes and your children's clothes, make lunches, and put everything you'll need for the day in your car. You'll rest easier knowing everything is all done.

Make Mornings Marvelous

Spend the last hour of the workday setting yourself up for success the next morning. Clear your desk of clutter, and file away any finished work to help tidy your space. Pull up the appointments and calls you need to make the next day, and then collect anything you need for those appointments. This way, even early morning emergencies will not derail you.

Start Slowly for Less Stress

When you start the day rushed, it adds to your stress level. Tension builds, making it a challenge to break out of that rushed feeling later in the day. Set your alarm early enough to give yourself time to eat breakfast and linger over a cup of coffee or tea while you read the paper or catch up on email. Giving yourself enough time gets your whole day off to a relaxed start.

Aromatherapy

Aromatherapy has been used for centuries all around the world. Many people turn to scent to improve their mood, health, and overall well-being. Now, members of our fast-paced society are rediscovering the natural benefits of aromatherapy in their everyday lives.

Smells can be used to help you relax or re-energize. For example, peppermint, ginger, and lemon can reinvigorate you, while lavender, jasmine, and vanilla relax you. Keep candles or scented potpourri around to soothe you and help mellow your mood.

Hyssop is mentioned in the Bible and is said to have healing properties to help with cold and flu. It can also be used to improve the skin and combat blemishes.

Basil is thought to help with concentration. It is also used to treat a wide variety of health conditions such as upset stomach, headaches, and flatulence.

Chamomile and nutmeg promote sleep, relaxation, and meditation. I drink a cup of chamomile tea nightly before bed.

Sandalwood has a very sweet, woody scent that brings relaxation and spiritual harmony. It also helps with dry hair and skin.

Many different types of roses have healing properties. Aside from soothing and calming, rose can also alleviate various skin problems.

Eucalyptus is a powerful decongestant used for centuries to help with cold symptoms. It also has antiseptic qualities.

Bid Bad Habits Bye-Bye

Limit caffeine to mornings, or go caffeine-free; high caffeine intake can leave you feeling tense or stressed. Work on going smoke-free as well, since cigarettes add to health woes and put a dent in your budget. While a glass of red wine a day is good for your heart,[4] keep in mind that alcohol is filled with empty calories, so moderation is key. Obesity stresses the body and raises your odds of getting cancer, diabetes, and a multitude of other diseases[5] which can also add to your stress levels. Start a sensible eating and exercise program to shed those extra pounds. What if you're only overweight? Shed those pounds anyway; it will be a fun health project!

Power Naps

A twenty-minute afternoon nap can jump-start your afternoon or evening. This will allow you to keep going for hours. Give yourself a break between work and home with a short nap. Remember, it's not selfish to ask your family for that time to make the transition.

Walk into Wonder

Decorate the portion of your house you first walk into when you arrive home. For me, this is the garage and the laundry room. For you, it may be the foyer. Wherever it is, make it pleasant enough that you smile. I painted the garage walls, put up small wallpaper bunches of flowers, and hung a painting in the laundry room, all of which make me happy. I remember telling someone I had hung these wallpaper flowers in the garage, and she was amazed. She probably thought I was nuts, but it worked for me.

Bubble Baths Bathe You in Bliss

One of my friends often says, "Float away in a sea of bubbles." I find this so true; some days, a long soak can change your life. Run a bubble bath, add music and aromatherapy candles, and voila—a spa day right at home. For the total experience, allow yourself to go on vacation from your troubles while your body relaxes. A half hour to an hour can literally make you feel like a new person and prepare you to face life's difficulties.

Massage Magic

Massages have great medicinal benefits. Treat yourself to a reflexology or hot stone massage. The pressure helps your body release toxins into your lymphatic system, so drink lots of water afterward to flush the toxins out and feel renewed.[7]

Pet Your Pet

Just owning a pet is a great way to add love and laughter to your life. For unconditional love, get a dog. For a more complicated relationship, get a cat. Studies have shown that petting your dog or cat can actually reduce your blood pressure. So go home and snuggle; your pet will enjoy it, and so will you.

If you don't currently have a pet, consider rescuing one from the shelter. You will be rescued right back.[8] Do keep in mind, however, that pets can add stress to a household. Dogs shed, bark, and need to be walked. Puppies, while adorable, may chew their way through your best shoes or some beloved furniture on their way to adulthood. Kittens are cuddly but need the litter changed, and they can also wreak havoc on clothes, furniture, and drapes with their tiny yet amazingly sharp claws. So think through the addition of pets carefully.

Fish Fantasies

It has been noted that blood pressure can actually be reduced by watching fish swim. (Also, fish can be a lot easier to take care of than shedding dogs or scratching cats.) Enjoy watching fish in a real aquarium, or get a DVD of ocean fish to relax.

Calendar Calm

Use your calendar to keep your life in perspective. Keep just one calendar for both work and home. This will keep you from overbooking. More importantly, on hectic days at work, it allows you to see you have some fun time planned as well.

A Three-Minute Vacation

When a real vacation is not possible, take a three-minute vacation. Put a vacation kit together with photos of your favorite travel spots and a playlist of favorite songs to load up while you dream for a moment, or simply take a spin through one of your vacation albums or on your phone or computer to relive the experience. Allow yourself to be transported and relax for three minutes. Do this with your loved one for extra fun.[9]

Colors Can Calm or Create Energy

Use color to set your mood. Oranges, reds, and yellows make you feel more energetic; blues and greens soothe; purples and pinks inspire creativity. Transform an area in your home into a mediation area where you can relax—a corner or an entire room, if you have space[10]

Music Mellows the Mood

Determine what kind of music soothes you most. Select some CDs with mellow music for those stressed-out days.[11] To relax, you may want to play classical, jazz, or a mix of nature and classical music. It makes great background music while you work. Keep it low for cubicle courtesy. Try some Mozart if you are working on mathematical problems such as paying the bills or balancing the checkbook; his music has been shown to improve math prowess. If you need inspiration or spiritual comfort, look to praise and worship CDs. They will bring much-needed peace.

> *1 Chronicles 15:16*
> *David told the leaders of the Levites to appoint their brothers as singers to sing joyful songs, accompanied by musical instruments: lyres, harps and cymbals.*

Picture Perfect

We all know we should take time to stop and smell the flowers. Why not stop and capture them on film while you're at it? Photography is a great hobby, encouraging one to take the time to appreciate nature's beauty: flowers, the sky, clouds, landscapes, or even one's own grandchildren. That can be a nice distraction from the stress and depressing issues whirling around you.

De-stress Any Activity

Look at any activity you hate doing and brainstorm ways to de-stress it. Do you hate paying bills? Add music, scented candles, or a cup of hot tea to de-stress the experience. Do you hate cooking? Purchase premade entrees to jazz up your meals. Do you hate mowing the lawn? Make a playlist of favorite tunes to listen to while mowing, or if you can afford it, hire the job out.

Ask a trusted friend to help you brainstorm if you are having trouble coming up with ways to de-stress your life. Your friend can also help hold you accountable in implementing your ideas.

Cloud Capers

As a child, I spent hours with my Aunt Carol. We lay on our backs, gazing at clouds and giggling about what we thought each one looked like—a rabbit, a bear, a man with a giant nose. It turns out research supports what we already knew. Counting clouds and imagining the images you see in them relaxes you and enhances your creativity.[12]

Bucolic Byways

Take the long way home. This often happens to me by accident, since I have zero sense of direction and rely on my GPS to guide me.

Sometimes I think the GPS senses my stress and decides to take me the scenic route, past cornfields or grazing cows. The newness of the route and the beauty of the scenery takes my mind off my troubles, and it keeps me focused on the now.

I've discovered there is actually a "detour" button on a Garmin GPS. (The button may vary depending on the brand.) It can reroute the driver to take longer but generally more scenic paths. Try choices such as "avoid highways," which forces the GPS to map out a route that's not on a major interstate. You can also ask your friends if they know any good roads for a scenic drive.

Curl Up with a Good Book

Read a good book to relax. You can go to a land far away, defeat dragons, solve murder mysteries, or learn about famous people. Add a cup of tea, light a fire, or play soft music in the background to really enjoy the experience.

Explore the Good Book

You may want to start exploring the Bible for comfort. The Psalms are a great place to find comfort.

> *Psalm 119:76*
> *May your unfailing love be my comfort,*
> *according to your promise to your servant.*

If you've never really read much of the Bible, you may want to start with the Gospel, the books of Matthew, Mark, Luke, and John. If you need encouragement, seek out the letters of Paul, Galatians, Ephesians, Philippians, or Colossians.

The apostle Paul wrote the next verse to his followers as he sat in jail.

> *Philippians 4:12*
> *I know what it is to be in need, and I know what it*
> *is to have plenty. I have learned the secret of being*
> *content in any and every situation, whether well*
> *fed or hungry, whether living in plenty or in want.*

Chapter Two Worksheet: Stress Buster Basics

What was the most powerful thought or strongest concept in this chapter for you?

_____

_____

_____

_____

If you implement one idea from this chapter, what would it be?

_____

_____

_____

_____

What do you plan to do differently as a result of what you read?

_____

_____

_____

_____

Which concept(s) would you like to share with family or friends?

_____

_____

_____

_____

*Allow God's love to flow through you
and relieve your stress.*

3. Exercise

1 Corinthians 6:19-20
Do you not know that your body is a
temple of the Holy Spirit, who is in you,
who you have received from God?

Add fun to exercise for maximum impact.

Physical Fitness

Take care of your body, and it will take care of you. Physical exercise improves your mood, combats disease, helps you manage your weight, strengthens your heart and lungs, and offers many other benefits. Severe stress can cause issues with our immune systems, making us more prone to illness.[1] Do monthly self-checks, get an annual physical, and take care of issues as they arise. The sooner you take care of medical problems, the easier and less stressful they are. The better shape you are in, the easier it is for you to care for your loved one.

18

Exercise Energizes

Exercise is the number one way to bust stress, as it reduces the adrenaline released in a stress event. Adding even small amounts of exercise can be beneficial, because activity produces endorphins. These handy peptides produce a rush of pleasure, which is more than enough reward for those who exercise even a little. It's assuredly a stress-buster. An article on *TheFamilyCaregiver.Org* states, "We need to guard against caregiver burnout and avoid becoming overly tired and exhausted, which can reduce our own body's ability to ward off illness. It is important to remember to create balance between caring for others and caring for ourselves."[2] Some easy tips to get more exercise include using stairs instead of the elevator, parking further away from the building and walking, using ten minutes of your lunch time to walk around the building, or walking up and down every aisle in the grocery store. Even walking around the mall or the Walmart is healthy mileage, and it adds to your total daily activity. Any or all of these little things add up to great ways to increase your exercise habits. Consider spending thirty to forty-five minutes a day walking outside or on a treadmill, or using another cardio machine such as an elliptical trainer, stair climber, or stationary bicycle.[3]

Relaxation Regimens

Deep breathing, visualization, progressive muscle relaxation, meditation, and yoga can all help you activate your relaxation response. Yoga provides both exercise and relaxation by combining exercise and music with deep breathing and meditation for an amazing overall experience. In addition to relaxation, each session will also give you increased stability and balance.

Relaxation techniques can reduce the stress caused by life's challenges; learning to relax can help you enjoy a better quality of life. Do some research to find relaxation techniques that work for you.[4]

Psalm 48:9
Within your temple, O God,
we meditate on your unfailing love.

Deep Breathing

Breathe in deeply and hold your breath while counting to six. Then slowly release your breath over another six-count. Repeat this several times. Don't you feel better already? Small breaths can limit the oxygen going into your body and can add more stress.[5] Often we do not breathe deeply enough to get the right amount of oxygen into our system. Oxygen, however, can demolish built-up stress hormones. Deep breathing is a great way to help the adrenaline released from stressors break down in a natural and positive way. Deep breathing can help alleviate anxiety arising from emotional turmoil. The calming, centering effects of deep breathing help us better cope with difficult situation.

Exodus 33:14
The Lord replied "My Presence will go
with you, and I will give you rest."

Chuck Swindall says, "God does not dispense strength and encouragement like a druggist who fills your prescription. The Lord doesn't promise to give us something to take so we can handle our weary moments. He promises us himself. That is all, and that is enough." [6]

Isaiah 55:6
Seek the Lord while he may be found,
call on him while he is near.

Chapter Three Worksheet: Exercise

What was the most powerful thought or strongest concept in this chapter for you?

_____

_____

_____

_____

If you implement one idea from this chapter, what would it be?

_____

_____

_____

_____

What do you plan to do differently as a result of what you read?

_____

_____

_____

_____

Which concept(s) would you like to share with family or friends?

_____

_____

_____

_____

Allow God's love to give you the strength to exercise your mind, body and spirit.

4. Eating Right

Eat wisely to live longer, healthier lives.

Antioxidant-Rich Foods

A recent study from the United States Department of Agriculture (USDA) analyzed food for antioxidant concentration and capacity per serving size. Cranberries, blueberries, and blackberries ranked highest among the fruits studied, while beans, artichokes, and russet potatoes topped the vegetable category. Of nuts, the best were pecans, walnuts, and hazelnuts.[1]

Although spices are generally consumed in small amounts, many are high in antioxidants. Ground cloves, ground cinnamon, and oregano scored the highest antioxidant concentrations among the spices studied.

Both the National Academy of Science (NAS) and the National Cancer Institute (NCI) advise eating at least five to nine servings of fruits and vegetables—that is, carotenoid—and antioxidant-rich foods—every day. But most people get only one or two. Try to fill your plate with color to get the widest variety and highest concentrations of these healthy vitamins and antioxidants: berries (blueberries, strawberries, raspberries, and blackberries), oranges, pink grapefruit, grapes, apricots, peaches, raisins, tomatoes, dark green leafy veggies (spinach, kale, and more), brussels sprouts, broccoli, beets, red peppers, and carrots.

Breakfast Builds a Better Body

There is no better start to the day than a good breakfast. The brain needs fuel to function. A heart-healthy cereal or oatmeal can provide an excellent option. Add a few blueberries, blackberries, raspberries, or strawberries for a dose of antioxidants.

You can also go the low-carb route and try hard or soft-boiled, poached, or scrambled eggs, or even go fancy and make an omelet. Personally, I cannot tell the difference between real eggs and low-cholesterol egg substitute products, so an egg-substitute or egg-white omelet tastes good to me.[2]

Lunch Lightens the Load

You may think working through lunch is a good idea, but it actually adds to your stress. By skipping lunch, you weaken your immune system, increase anxiety, and increase your level of distractions. Taking even fifteen minutes to relax and eat lunch is a needed break. Allow yourself that time.

If the weather remains pretty, go outside and eat to get a little natural vitamin D from the sun. Try a spinach salad with blueberries, blackberries, raspberries, or strawberries for another shot of antioxidants. Drink white tea or green tea to really boost your immune system.

It may help to eat several small meals throughout the day. Try to grab a quick, healthy bite, such as yogurt or fruit, a couple of hours after breakfast. Getting five to seven small meals helps you eat smaller portions and feel full longer. A steady flow of healthy, energizing food also keeps the metabolism up.

Dark Chocolate Delivers

Do you need an excuse to eat chocolate? Dark chocolate has naturally occurring antidepressants. It is suggested to eat one to two ounces of dark chocolate a day. Milk chocolate has some, and white chocolate has none.[3] So when depressed, reach for the dark chocolate. I recently discovered pomegranate seeds covered in dark chocolate. With that snack, you get antioxidants wrapped in an antidepressant—and a lovely taste sensation, too![4]

Tea Time Totally Transforms You

A cup of herbal tea can soothe your spirit and add antioxidants to your system. Taking time to enjoy tea while meditating or listening to soothing music adds extra benefits. It gives you a much-needed five to ten-minute break to rest and reenergize. White tea has the highest levels of antioxidants, followed by green tea, and then black tea.

Herbal infusions can also provide comfort and rejuvenation, although their antioxidant content depends on the herbs used to brew them. At night, I personally love Tension Tamer Tea by Celestial Seasonings. It has a lovely taste, and it is a very relaxing blend of eleuthero ginseng, ginger root, and chamomile.

Water Works

Drinking eight glasses of water a day is a good way to flush toxins from your system; it also keeps you hydrated and feeling full. If you do not like the taste of plain water, add a touch of lemon or lime juice.[5] Vitamin-enhanced waters with antioxidants are now on the market too; just watch the sugar content before downing too many.

Protein Packs a Punch

Go for snacks that are high in protein but not in sugar. The sugar makes you feel better for a short time, but then you crash. Yogurt, cheese, and nuts such as almonds are high in protein and a powerful afternoon snack.[6]

Proverbs 3:7-8
Do not be wise in your own eyes;
fear the Lord, and shun evil.
This will bring health to your body
and nourishment to your bones.

Chapter Four Worksheet: Eating Right

What was the most powerful thought or strongest concept in this chapter for you?

_____
_____
_____
_____

If you implement one idea from this chapter, what would it be?

_____
_____
_____
_____

What do you plan to do differently as a result of what you read in this chapter?

_____
_____
_____
_____

Which concept(s) would you like to share with family or friends?

_____
_____
_____
_____

Allow God's love to make you crave the foods that will soothe your soul and strengthen your body.

5. Laugh It Up

Friends are the gift you give yourselves.

Laughter Livens Life

Take time to laugh. Play with children, chat with friends, read the funnies, watch comedies, or just force yourself to laugh about nothing. Whatever makes you laugh is a good thing. It gets oxygen into your system and energizes you.[1]

> **Psalm 126:2**
> *Our mouths were filled with laughter,*
> *our tongues with songs of joy. Then it*
> *was said among the nations, "The Lord*
> *has done great things for them."*

Laughter is a healing activity: it can boost your immune system, act as a pain reliever by releasing endorphins (the body's natural painkillers), aide indigestion, and increase lung capacity.[2] Dr. Caricioni would say he really liked it when Dave and I would make jokes and tease while in his office as he said it made the treatment work more effectively.

In *The Five Habits of Health Transformation*, Mike Adams states that laughter can counteract the negative effects chronic stress has on a caretaker's health.[3]

> ***Job 8:21***
> ***He will yet fill your mouth with laughter***
> ***and your lips with shouts of joy.***

Cook Up Fun

Cook up some fun with your children, and allow them to help. Make a "dirt cake" using gummy worms, or make s'mores over a fire in the backyard. Look for ways to have fun in the kitchen with your children or friends.

> ***Zechariah 14:21***
> ***Every pot in Jerusalem and Judah will be holy to***
> ***the Lord Almighty, and all who come to sacrifice***
> ***will take some of the pots and cook in them.***

Play Time

Take time out to joke and play. Play with your coworkers, your family, and strangers standing in line. Look for ways to make others laugh and smile. You'll laugh and smile with them—a win-win situation.

Friends Foster Fun

Have a get-together with friends. Make it a potluck or have everyone meet at a restaurant. You needn't have a clean house or a do lot of prep work. Even a short visit with friends can provide tremendous spiritual refreshment, stress relief, and renewed strength.

> ***Proverbs 18:24***
> ***A man of many companions may come to ruin, but***
> ***there is a friend who sticks closer than a brother.***

Creativity Inspires

Creating something new and fun will release your inner artist and make you feel inspired. Paint a room, complete a painting, make a piece of furniture, do a flower arrangement, or try your hand at photography. Just do something creative. As Ray Bradbury said, "Don't think. Thinking is the enemy of creativity. It's self-conscious, and anything self-conscious is lousy. You can't try to do things. You simply must do things."[4]

Keep a notebook with you; when you spend time waiting at various doctor appointments, you can jot down your creative ideas or write poetry.

Hide Away in Hollywood

Movies can be a great way to distract you for hours. Something about going to the theater and enjoying the big screen experience really does transport you to faraway times and places.[5] Try comedies to invoke laughter and lightheartedness. Grab a friend, or go by yourself. Just remember to go light at the concession stand; buttered popcorn, candy, and soda just weigh you down.

Write the Wit

Both my mother and Dave said some very funny things during their long illnesses. Mostly this was thanks to the prescription drugs they were taking at the time, but I still laugh thinking about them. Keep a log of these verbal gems. It will remind you that humor and wit can win out, even in the darkest hours.

For example, my mother and father had taken numerous cruises. One day in her very small nursing room, my mother looked around and said, "I do not know who invited me on this cruise, but I am *so* not having a good time." After we quit laughing, we volunteered to talk to the "cruise director" for her.

Journaling Joys

Journaling is an excellent way to vent, explore your emotions, and get in touch with the inner you.[6] Ladies, buy yourselves a pretty blank book for journaling. Men, there are great leather books out there that will let you feel very masculine while you journal. Pick a time of day that works for you. This way you can be consistent, and you have a better chance of keeping it up. Later you will be able to go back and watch yourself evolve. You can choose a particular focus such as journaling specific things you are grateful for. You can also journal the moments where you see God working in your life or how you see God working through you. For example when he answers a prayer.

Ephesians 2:10
For we are God's workmanship, created
in Christ Jesus to do good works, which
God prepared in advance for us to do.

Mattie Stepanek (July 17, 1990-June 22, 2004), a young man suffering from dysautonomic mitochondrial myopathy, wrote numerous books of poetry. In interviews, he said that what mattered to him was "praying and playing, and celebrating life every day in some way." Mattie's motto was to "think gently, speak gently, live gently." He was famous for saying, "Remember to play after every storm."[7]

Say Hi to Natural Highs

Remember there are lots of natural highs you can get from life if you work to live in the now. Here are a few:

1. Be thankful for God's grace
2. Be with people you love
3. Laugh so hard your face hurts or your drink comes out your nose
4. A long, hot shower
5. See God's guiding hand in your life
6. No lines at the supermarket
7. Close parking spaces
8. A gorgeous flower in bloom
9. Real mail from a real friend
10. A leisurely drive down a country road
11. Your favorite song on the radio
12. Rain on the roof
13. Hot towels fresh out of the dryer
14. Your favorite flavor of milkshake
15. A leisurely bubble bath
16. Giggling
17. A good conversation
18. A walk on the beach
19. Watch children play
20. Play with your grandchildren
21. Find a twenty dollar bill in a pocket Laugh at yourself
22. Look into someone's eyes and know they love you
23. Midnight phone calls that last for hours
24. Running through sprinklers

25. Laughing for absolutely no reason
26. Having someone tell you that you are beautiful
27. An inside joke with friends
28. Accidentally overhearing someone say something nice about you
29. To wake up and realize you still have a few hours left to sleep
30. Your first kiss (either the very first one or the first one with a new partner)
31. Make new friends or to spend time with old ones
32. Play with a new puppy or kitten
33. A foot or hand massage
34. Watch cloud formations and make up stories about what they are
35. Sweet dreams
36. Hot chocolate or tea
37. Sit outside and listen to the birds sing sweet melodies
38. Ice cream on a hot summer day
39. Hit the sweet spot on your golf club or tennis racket
40. Popcorn and cocoa on a cold winter night
41. Road trips with friends
42. Swing on swings
43. Make eye contact with a cute stranger
44. Homemade cookies such as chocolate chip
45. Hold hands with someone you care about
46. An old friend
47. Watch the expression on someone's face as they open a much-desired present from you
48. A sunrise or sunset
49. Get out of bed every morning and know the day is going to be beautiful
50. Knowing that somewhere right now somebody misses you and is thinking sweet thoughts about you
51. A hug from someone you care about deeply
52. Knowing you have done the right thing no matter what other people think
53. Do a random act of kindness for a stranger
54. Do an anonymous act of kindness for a friend
55. Bubble baths with candles
56. Rereading a favorite book
What are your favorite things?

Feel free to copy some of mine, but only if they give you that natural high too!

_____

_____

_____

Ecclesiastes 3:2–8
A time to be born and a time to die;
A time to plant, and a time to uproot;
A time to kill and a time to heal;
A time to tear down and a time to build;
A time to weep, and a time to laugh;
A time to mourn and a time to dance;
A time to scatter stones and a time to gather them;
A time to embrace, and a time to refrain;
A time to search and a time to give up;
A time to keep, and a time to throw away;
A time to tear, and a time to mend;
A time to be silence, and a time to speak;
A time to love, and a time to hate;
A time for war, and a time for peace.

Crying Can Calm

When you are stressed, frustrated, or angry, crying it out can be very therapeutic.[8] The old saying says the world laughs with you, but you cry alone. This does not have to be true, though. If you want to cry, go ahead and cry. My friends have all seen me cry over the last three years, and they have all been very supportive.

"Often, people report that a good cry can make them feel better and more at peace. Victor Parachin's book "Fears about Tears? Why Crying is Good for You discusses a survey where 85 percent of women and 73 percent of men reported feeling less sad or angry after crying."[9] As a result of this kind of information, psychologists and scientists are doing research to discover what the content and purpose of tears may be. William Frey conducted research in an effort to discover the chemical makeup of tears. Frey compared tears of sadness with tears caused by cutting a raw onion. He found the tears that resulted from emotional stimuli contained more total protein than those resulting from irritation.

Frey proposed that the emotional tears contained high levels of cortisol, which is a primary stress hormone. This suggests that we may be literally releasing toxins from our system when we cry, and that crying itself may support our overall well-being. That definitely made me feel better about crying! Sure, I wanted to "stay strong," but I liked knowing that my tears released toxins that needed to escape anyway.

Psychologists intuitively understand the healing power of tears and often encourage people to cry freely, uninhibited by any internal sensors.[10] Best friends who let you cry or who cry with you—rather than the ones who get frustrated or freaked out—provide much-needed support at those tough times.

Song Soothes the Soul

When your favorite song comes on the radio, do you ever get transported back to a certain time and place? Song is the language of the soul.[11] God gave us songs to sing in Psalms.

For me, the song that best captured what I was feeling during the year of Dave's illness was Jo Dee Messina's "Bring on the Rain." Almost every evening, on the way home from work, I'd play this and sing my heart out. Often tears streamed down my cheeks, but at the end of the song, I felt stronger and more in charge. Pick a theme song for your journey and let the heavens hear your song.

Chapter Five Worksheet: Laugh It Up

What was the most powerful thought or strongest concept in this chapter for you?

_____
_____
_____
_____

If you implement one idea from this chapter, what would it be?

_____
_____
_____
_____

What do you plan to do differently as a result of what you read?

_____
_____
_____
_____

Which concept(s) would you like to share with family or friends?

_____
_____
_____
_____

*Allow God's love to help you see His grace
and the goodness in His world.*

6. Focus on the Present

"Yesterday is a memory.
Tomorrow is all possibility.
Today is a gift; that's why they call it the present.
Live in the now."
—Alice Morse Earle

"The future will depend on what we do in the present."
—Mahatma Gandhi

Skydiving was on my bucket list.

A Now Focus

I grew up watching the 1946 movie *It's a Wonderful Life* every holiday season. It made you wonder what your life really means. Similarly, *The Bucket List*, starring Jack Nicholson and Morgan Freeman, is a movie that leaves you thinking about the components of your life and how you want to live your life "in the now." Consider making your own "bucket list" of things you want to do or experience before you proverbially kick the bucket. Rent the movie. It is thought provoking.

Focus on the now—being alive, awake, and alert in the moment of *now*. Start thinking about the memories you want to make with your children, friends, and grandchildren.[1] Remember, "life is not measured by the number of breaths we take but by the number of moments that take your breath away" (author unknown).

Of course, I felt Dave passed from this Earth way too soon at sixty. However, we both had the opportunity to travel abroad and do amazing things: watch a sunrise in Italy, walk the Gap of Dunloe in Ireland, canoe in Costa Rica, get up close and personal with elephants is Botswana, and fish for piranha in the Amazon. We weren't aware of our own mortality in each of those moments, but I'm glad we did such a good job of living in the present.

1 Timothy 6:19
In this way they will lay up treasure for themselves as a firm foundation for the coming age, so that they may take hold of the life that is truly life.

Family Time

Allow yourself to spend time with your family. Have dinner together. Pick one night a week for game night. Take your teens out to dinner with their friends once a month, or even double-date with them. Go on a family vacation and leave all the electronics at home. Visit older family members and reminisce; try to capture the memories on digital film or video.[2]

Make Magical Memories

When faced with a terminal illness, start thinking about how to make great memories for your children or grandchildren. Go to the zoo, visit museums, take a family trip, hold regular game nights: you will be making memories that will outlast you and your loved one. Our kids were wonderful; they made regular car trips from Chicago to Topeka for weekend visits so we could see our grandchildren. It was an amazing blessing.

1 Timothy 5:8
If anyone does not provide for his relatives, and especially for his immediate family, he has denied the faith and is worse than an unbeliever.

Hobbies Help

Hobbies give us a break from reality; along with the chance to indulge our sense of play, we also get to reduce stress levels.[3] When you're stressed, take time out for your favorite activity, whether gardening, walking, horseback riding, painting, playing computer games, flying kites, or driving in the country. Anything that gives you a little time away from the constant stress of illness or other life stressors will be time well spent.

Hobbies can also provide an outlet to meet people and develop relationships with others who may offer you support. Look into knitting groups, book clubs, or amateur painting courses to feed both your mind and soul.

Ecclesiastes 3:1
There is a time for everything, and a
season for every activity under heaven.

Nature and Nurture

Take time out to enjoy the world around you. Take a walk; sit and listen to the trees rustle in the wind; let the sun shine on your face. You'll be amazed at how relaxing it is to just sit back and enjoy all the natural sounds around you. Take your lunch outside, or go to the park on the weekend and watch the children play. There is something very restful and peaceful about allowing nature to nurture you. It reenergizes your spirit and gets your vitamin D levels recharged so you keep your bones healthy.[4]

Treat Yourself

What do you consider a true treat? Getting a facial, going rock climbing, having a pedicure, or visiting a casino? Do it once in a while. In the chart, list the things you consider treats, and describe how they impact you. Consider your budget, as you do not want to add stress by blowing too much money, but also keep in mind that there are budget-friendly versions of these treats (such as using cosmetology schools for facials or hosting a casino night in your basement). When you are under the constant stress of having a seriously ill loved one, you need an occasional treat, and you shouldn't feel guilty for the indulgence.[5]

Treat	When Did You Do It?	Impact?
Facial	Once a month	Very relaxing

Chapter Six Worksheet: Focus on the Present

What was the most powerful thought or strongest concept in this chapter for you?

_____

_____

_____

_____

If you implement one idea from this chapter, what would it be?

_____

_____

_____

_____

What do you plan to do differently as a result of what you read?

_____

_____

_____

_____

Which concept(s) would you like to share with family or friends?

_____

_____

_____

_____

Allow God's love to help you focus on your blessings rather than your trials.

7. Adjust Your Attitude

Serenity is a state of mind – not a place.

Gratitude Attitude

Lou Holtz said, "It is not what happens to you that counts. It is how you react to what happens to you."

I totally agree. While I haven't always handled things the way I'd like, I work to keep my life in perspective. The more you can focus on the good things you still have left and that are still happening around you, the better you will be able to cope.

Author Melody Bettie once said, "Gratitude unlocks the fullness of life. It turns what we have into enough and more. It turns denial into acceptance, chaos into order, and confusion to clarity. It can turn a meal into a feast, a house into a home, or a stranger into a friend. Gratitude makes sense of the past, brings peace for today, and creates vision for the morrow."

I started a gratitude journal when I had cancer to help me focus on the good in every day. I started another one the day after Dave passed away. It helped me maintain my sanity. A journal might help you as well. Just jot down one to three things each day for which you are grateful, and then thank God that night for His mercy and blessings.

Proverbs 15:30
A cheerful look brings joy to the heart, and
good news gives health to the bones.

Attitude Adjustments

Adjust how you think of a task to make it less stressful.[1] If you consider weeding to be torture, it will be. If you think of it as your personal time to commune with nature or God, it becomes a stress-busting activity. If you start calling those gruesome tasks "playtime," it'll change your perspective. When you do yard work, focus on how amazing the world is in all its glory. I often think of weeds as the toxins I need to eliminate from my body or as people I don't like. Then I take pleasure in removing them from the landscape. When you do dishes, try reminiscing about the joyous family time that got them dirty in the first place.

Philippians 4:13
I can do everything through Him
who gives me strength.

Attitude of Gratitude

Cultivate an "attitude of gratitude." Appreciate that your loved one has been with you as long as he or she has; rather than focusing on being left, focus on what you have learned from knowing and loving him or her. Love is a rare gift indeed, and we do not often find it. The fact you have experienced it is a true blessing.[2]

Philippians 4:8
Finally, brothers, whatever is true, whatever is
noble, whatever is right, whatever is pure, whatever
is lovely, whatever is admirable—if anything is
excellent or praiseworthy—think about such things.

The things I admire about my loved one:	The things I learned from my loved one:	The things I would like to communicate to my loved one:
Ex. His quick wit and intelligence	Ex. Not to stress when I lose something but to relax and retrace my steps mentally before doing it physically	Ex. How lucky I was to find him

Conquer Your Commute

Most of us spend significant time commuting. Look for ways to conquer your commute. Why not turn valuable time into a useful resource? Check out some audio books from your library and learn something new, or try a new genre of music: rock out with heavy metal, relax with jazz, mellow with classical, or worship and calm your soul with Christian songs.

Trying a new route to or from work can spice things up. Also, adding a new beverage while you drive can make it more fun. I've grown fond of vanilla lattes, and I try every distributor's version for comparison tastings.

If you know others who make the same commute, consider carpooling. Sharing a chore like a commute can become an enjoyable social experience. Or, if you have the option, take public transportation. Doing so eliminates driving stress, plus it helps the environment. If you can bicycle or walk, shorter commutes become exercise (and an opportunity to save gas money). Finally, you may be able to ask your boss and human resources department for the option of telecommuting one day a week.

Reward Your Hard Work

Look at your to-do list for the most fun task. Then use it as a reward (or bribe) for finishing tasks you must do but don't relish.[3] Try to find rewards that are good for you, like taking a walk, giving yourself time to spend with a friend, or doing something nice for someone else. Try not to use food rewards—you'll just need to join a gym to work off the extra pounds!

For example, I hate ironing and love working on the computer, so editing this book was a much more fun task than ironing the laundry. I used editing as a reward for getting the drudge work of ironing done. When I was trying hard to lose weight, I used my love of jewelry to motivate myself into walking two and a half miles a day. When I walked one hundred miles, I got to go jewelry shopping, and when I got to two hundred fifty miles, I got to go again! It worked, and I lost the weight I needed to lose. I also got some lovely new jewels.

Are you still having trouble with your attitude? Don't beat yourself up. There are days when mine is certainly less than stellar. Read the verse below and think through how to be less anxious and more grateful. I recently read a great book, *Calm My Anxious Heart*, by Linda Dillow, that helped me with these issues; I highly recommend it.

> *Philippians 4:6–7*
> *Do not be anxious about anything, but in everything, by prayer and petition, with thanksgiving, present your request in God. And the peace of God, which transcends all understanding, will guard your hearts and your minds in Christ Jesus.*

Chapter Seven Worksheet: Adjust your Attitude

What was the most powerful thought or strongest concept in this chapter for you?

_____

_____

_____

_____

If you implement one idea from this chapter, what would it be?

_____

_____

_____

_____

What do you plan to do differently as a result of what you read?

_____

_____

_____

_____

Which concept(s) would you like to share with family or friends?

_____

_____

_____

_____

Allow God's love to give you an attitude of praise and thanksgiving each and every day.

8. Get Focused: Preparing for the Long Haul

Be persistent. Water will even wear rock down over time.

Prioritizing Is Power

Review your to-do list, and highlight the items that must get done right away. Use a colored marker or a highlighter so you can easily see them when you look at the list. Focus on getting those top items done. Remember the eighty/twenty rule, which is that twenty percent of what you do will get you eighty percent of the results.[1]

Even if you get just five of twenty-five things accomplished, you can feel less stressed and more successful if they were the *right* five things. For example, your top five for the day might be spending quality time with your loved one, sending something fun to a far-away friend, praying, taking your loved one to a doctor appointment, and exercising.

> *Titus 3:8*
> *This is a trustworthy saying. And I want you to stress these things, so that those who have trusted in God may be careful to devote themselves to doing what is good. These things are excellent and profitable for everyone.*

Ditch or Switch Duties

Evaluate the committees, boards, and other volunteer work you do. Then determine what you should ditch and what you should switch. You have the perfect excuse to resign from some of the commitments that really zap time but are not part of your personal mission for you and your loved one.

It's fine to beg off current assignments or get replacements for yourself on long-term committees or boards. Let people know what's going on in your life and why you need to step down from the committee or board. This allows them to get someone else switched into your role, which is much better than you doing the assignments poorly or not at all. In the long run, your reputation will be protected rather than harmed.

Divvy Up the Duties

If children are still in your home, get them to help out. They need to learn responsibility, and they will best learn through helping you with chores. Divvy up the duties around the house so not everything falls to you. Look for ways to make the duties fun. For example, rev up the music and rock out while you clean. Picking up their things feels like a game when they're racing against the clock to see who can do it fastest! Or let your kids dress in costume for dinner after they have set the table.

> *Acts 20:35*
> *In everything I did, I showed you that by this kind of hard work we must help the weak,*

> *remembering the words the Lord Jesus himself
> said: "It is more blessed to give than to receive."*

Clear the Clutter

Begin to clear the clutter from your life, one drawer or closet at a time. Sort things into what you want to keep and what you know other family members want. Sell or donate the rest.[2] The "I Sold It" stores make eBay easy, but they do take a hefty percentage of the profit for their convenience. If you have more time, sell things on eBay yourself. You can also sell via consignment at various antique or other stores; Goodwill, your local homeless shelter, or church organizations providing support for abused women and children are always looking for household items.

Keep a list of what you donate so you can claim the deductions on your taxes.[3] If you are like me, you will find it emotionally freeing to clear up space. If you will ultimately need to downsize, it gets the process of uncluttering under way so it will not be overwhelming when the time comes.

Optimize Organization

It's stressful when you cannot find what you need when you need it. Take time to get yourself organized. Establish a place for keys, cell phones, and other frequently used items. Set up your desktop for easy access to what you need most often, and organize both your paper and computer files for easy access. Tackle one drawer or closet at a time so you are not overwhelmed. I found it much easier to downsize my dad's belongings while he was still alive than I did my mom's things after she passed away. It was less of an emotional drain.[4]

Delegate

If you are in a leadership role at your job, begin delegating even more. Delegating tasks grooms your staff and develops their talents; it's actually a sign of good leadership skills. Look at the repetitive tasks on your to-do list, and determine which of your direct reports could be trained to take them over. Train that person, and then delegate those tasks permanently.[5]

You may also want to hire a maid, nurse's aide, or other person to help around the house during this time. Becoming a "boss" in your home comes with new responsibilities. Look at your renter's or homeowner's insurance to be certain you are covered if a hired helper in your home causes an accident or is injured. Also remember to make sure your hired help is legally allowed to work in the United States. You can obtain and fill out a copy of an I-9 form and keep it in the employee's file.[6]

Scheduling Success

Guard your schedule at work and home to keep it from becoming too tight. Allow ten to fifteen minutes between meetings or appointments so if one runs late, you can still make the next one on time. Leave at least one hour a day for doing actual work; when you book meetings solid, you feel overwhelmed at the end of the day, usually because you haven't actually accomplished any of your tasks. Make sure you allot the time required for the things that must get done.

Swap Shop or Job Share

If you have an assignment you don't enjoy, find a colleague or neighbor who does enjoy it and swap. For example, perhaps you could do a colleague's calculations and charts if he or she writes your proposal. On the home front, maybe you can mow the lawn for a neighbor, and he or she could cook for you. It can be a win–win situation that's less stressful for both of you.

Another option is job-sharing. Talk to your human resource department to determine if you could share your job with a coworker in order to take time off more easily. Don't forget you will likely qualify for time off through the Family Medical Leave Act. Explore your options.[7]

> *Philemon 1:17*
> *So if you consider me a partner, welcome*
> *him as you would welcome me.*

Potluck Meals

If everyone is coming for dinner or the weekend, have each bring something fun to share. Allow yourself to enjoy the company of others and share food and fun together without all the work. Friends, neighbors, and church members may offer to help feed you; accept their generosity. I know I would not have survived without my circle of friends during the most stressful times.

1 Chronicles 12:40
Also, their neighbors from as far away as
Issachar, Zebulun, and Naphtali came,
bringing food on donkeys, camels, mules
and oxen. There were plentiful supplies of
flour, fig cakes, raisin cakes, wine, oil, cattle
and sheep, for there was joy in Israel.

Partner for Progress with a Circle of Friends

It is okay to ask for help. Your friends want to help; they just don't necessarily know what you need or how best to assist. Have friends and neighbors bring meals, assist with transportation, help with cleaning, or do other chores so you can focus more of your time on your loved one.[8]

If your loved one requires constant care, ask friends to come by so you can get a break. Even if it's just long enough to get your hair done, grocery shop, or run some personal errands, it can be a huge help. Using an Internet-based system like Caring Bridge can help everyone stay informed, and it allows you to coordinate who is doing what and what tasks still need to be done.

It's also great to simply enjoy the company of your friends. Ask them to come over for a meal or a chat. There is huge value in sharing time with people who are supportive of you. A shared burden becomes lighter, and sharing with trustworthy friends can be very therapeutic.

It is important when you hear the question, "Is there anything I can do to help?" that there is one answer: "Yes."[9] The help of others is key, and it can help de-stress your life.

1 John 7-9
Dear friends, let us love one another, for love
comes from God. Everyone who loves has
been born of God and knows God. Whoever
does not love does not know God, because
God is love. This is how God showed his love
among us: He sent his one and only Son into
the world that we might live through him.

Chapter Eight Worksheet: Get Focused

What was the most powerful thought or strongest concept in this chapter for you?

_____

_____

_____

_____

If you implement one idea from this chapter, what would it be?

_____

_____

_____

_____

What do you plan to do differently as a result of what you read?

_____

_____

_____

_____

Which concept(s) would you like to share with family or friends?

_____

_____

_____

_____

Allow God's love to flow through you and focus you on the important things in life.

9. Reach Outside Yourself

You only get the beauty of a rainbow after the rain.

Spread Joy on the Go

In the midst of your difficulty, look for ways to have some fun and spread joy to others everywhere you go.[1] Take something fun like cookies or little flowers to the other patients at chemotherapy. You needn't spend a lot; go to the Dollar Store or Walmart so you won't break the bank while spreading joy. Also consider giving gifts to the nursing staff who care so diligently for your loved one. You'll make them smile, and you'll smile in return.

Volunteer

Any time you focus on others who are worse off, it gives you some perspective. My neighbor and best friend exemplifies this. She has taken on not only me, but several other friends, as her "projects." Her husband had cancer, but he went into remission while Dave was severely ill. She ministered to my husband and me during the medical crisis.

Volunteering allows you to help others and make a positive difference.[2] Choose an organization that resonates with you and get active. Find a person to help. If each one of us helped just one other person, it would be a better world.

> *Ecclesiastes 4:10*
> *If one falls down, his friend can help*
> *him up. But pity the man who falls*
> *and has no one to help him up.*

Joyful Thanks

Strive to write a thank-you note to a colleague or friend every day. Watch it alleviate his or her stress and yours at the same time. You'll cultivate an "attitude of gratitude" while developing and deepening your relationships. I love receiving thank-you notes, so I know how much they mean to others.

Save the thank-you notes you receive. If you have a down day, go back and reread them. You'll realize the joy you brought to others. Set out to do something "thank-you-noteworthy." In giving to others, you give a gift to yourself: self-esteem. If you really want to have some fun, do it anonymously. Afterward, sit back and watch the joy and wonder an anonymous donation or gift creates.

> *2 Timothy 1:3*
> *... I thank God for you—the God I serve with a*
> *clear conscience, just as my ancestors did. Night*
> *and day I constantly remember you in my prayers.*

Chapter Nine Worksheet: Reach Outside Yourself

What are your "thank-you-noteworthy" deeds?

_____
_____
_____

What was the most powerful thought or strongest concept in this chapter for you?

_____
_____
_____

If you implement one idea from this chapter, what would it be?

_____
_____
_____

What do you plan to do differently as a result of what you read in this chapter?

_____
_____
_____

Which concept(s) would you like to share with family or friends from this chapter?

_____
_____
_____

*Allow God's love to shine as it flows
from you to others!*

10. Take Action . . . Now

Rome was not built in a day; neither is your life.

Pick Your Problems Off

Focus on solving problems rather than being overwhelmed. Use the flower petals technique, which helps you deal with problems and take action. In the center of each flower, list your problem. On each petal, brainstorm a potential solution to the problem. Then start weeding your problems one by one. Pick a flower and a solution each day, and get it solved. You will feel empowered every time you actually solve a problem.

For example, if your car is in need of major repairs, put the word "car" in the middle of the flower. Next, start brainstorming the options: you can get it fixed, buy a new one, see if someone would loan you one for a while, or buy a used one. If it is a second car, you could do without for a while. Now that you have your options, get costs for each and decide which you want to do.

Now it's your turn!

Draw some flowers, and jot a problem or challenge in the center of the flower. Then jot ideas for solving it in each petal.

Worries Be Gone

A high percentage of what you worry about will never happen. Prove it to yourself.

> *Matthew 6:27*
> *Who of you by worrying can add*
> *a single hour to his life?*

Get a piece of paper and write your worries of the month down. Once you're done, put the paper away, and jot down on your calendar when you're going to look at it. At the end of the month, reflect on how many of your worries actually came to pass. I'm betting very few actually did. This exercise will help you prove it to yourself.

When you start to worry, ask yourself how likely it is that the worry is real. If the likelihood is high, then do something to prevent or lessen the worry. Taking action gives you control. For example, if you are worried about spur-of-the-moment ER visits, pack a bag for each of you and prepare a list of medications, just in case.

Do not waste time with worry; we are only here in this life for a short visit. Make your moments count. Learn to live in the now.

> *Philippians 4:11*
> *I am not saying this because I am in*
> *need, for I have learned to be content*
> *whatever the circumstances.*

The word "content" in Greek is *autarkies,* and it means "self-sufficient." The ancient stories use the word "content" to mean self-reliance, fortitude, and a calm acceptance of life's pressures. The apostle Paul, however, used it to refer to a divinely bestowed sufficiency. When Paul was in prison and facing death, he wrote Timothy to encourage him.

Popular teacher and speaker Beth Moore says the word "content" means *to be enough for a thing.* When our mind is focused on God and our trust in Him, we can be at perfect peace, even when the world around us rages.

This is a tough concept to practice. I often have to remind myself to find contentment in the now and not wish my life away or grouse about what is happening. I totally understand the challenge of being content regardless of what I have. Sometimes it helps me to sit and realize that so many people have it much worse than myself.

> *Isaiah 26:3–4*
> *You will keep in perfect peace Him whose*
> *mind is steadfast, because He trusts in*
> *you. Trust in the Lord forever, for the*
> *Lord, the Lord, is the Rock eternal.*

Do the Three-Step

There is a three-step process to eliminate stress from your day-to-day existence.[4] I have provided a chart below that has the three steps. Go ahead and fill out a few boxes; you'll be less stressed in no time.

For example, I am not a morning person, and I was always running late. So I took charge of the situation and made a few changes that really have helped over the years. For one, I lay out my clothes the night before. It takes me much less time to make that decision in the evening than in the morning when I'm brain-dead. I also wear my hair in a short cut that takes very little time to do, and I have streamlined my makeup routine to almost no time. Now I can go from the shower to the office in under twenty minutes.

Step 1. Identify a stressor.	Step 2. Determine what you could do to reduce, change, or eliminate it.	Step 3. Take action.
Time it takes to get ready in the morning	Options: 1. Lay clothes out the night before 2. Get up a few minutes earlier 3. Get a shorter hair cut that takes less time	Actions: Lay out my clothes the night before. Get the shorter haircut.

Make Little Moments Monumental

Work to make the time you have together more fun and more special. Start having breakfast on the deck while listening to the birds chirp. Light candles and use your wedding china and crystal for dinner, even if it is a chicken potpie or warmed-up mac and cheese. Do your telecommuting on the back deck while you watch the squirrels. Look for ways to make the little moments more monumental and magical.

Mark the God Moments

I don't know about you, but there are times in my life I look back and definitely see the hand of God. Maybe it's a perfect event, a person who came into your life at just the right time, or a sermon delivered just when you needed it most. These are what I call "God moments." One of my friends calls them "miracle moments." It doesn't matter what you call them, but do make an effort to notice them. Start tracking them. They are not always easy to see when they are happening.

Sometimes God says no to your prayer. Maybe the God moment appears tragic or just plain wrong at the time. Later you will realize it was a good thing after all, and it was part of the grand plan. I wanted children of my very own, but I could never have them. Then I met a man, Dave, who had two wonderful sons, and I was lucky to be their stepmom or "second mother," as we called it. God didn't give me children of my own, but that meant I could focus on my stepchildren when they came into my life. A friend of mine had Stage IV cancer for some time. He said his walk with God was greatly enhanced by his disease, and so was his marriage. He served as a true inspiration to so many others as they watched his journey and trust in God's will.

At work, we often assist outplaced staff in finding new careers. I am always surprised at how many look back later and say being let go was the best thing that ever happened to them. It forced them to reevaluate their careers, or it gave them the push to start their own companies. For some, it even gave them the opening to move where they always wanted.

I've had several God moments throughout my life. When I was dealing with cancer myself, I met Sue in one of the classes I was teaching. She was bald and wore giant earrings. I knew, like me, she was on chemotherapy. We chatted at a break, and I found out she had been given three months to live … fourteen years before. Yet she was still very much alive: she was working on getting a doctorate while employed full-time, and she also volunteered with other cancer patients. God put her in my path to give me hope. Sue is gone now, but she inspired many, including me.

Sometimes, it's all about timing. We had a piece of property that had been for sale for over two years. No one had showed the slightest interest at all. One month before Dave passed away, we got an offer on it, and the property closed just before Dave went into hospice care. The money from the sale paid for all the final expenses we incurred.

Also, in sixteen years, we had never had anyone ask about buying our family-run business. In December of 2007, about a month before Dave was diagnosed with cancer, someone asked us about selling the business to them in 2008. We declined. In February of 2008, Dave was diagnosed and given less than six months to live. We re-contacted the couple and arranged the sale. To me, this was also God's hand at work. He was sending us just what we needed when we needed it. I was able to sell the business two weeks after Dave passed away.

Another God moment happened when I was feeling very lonely at night after Dave went to sleep. The next morning, David and I were having breakfast at Perkins. As we walked to our car, we heard a plaintive mewl. Upon investigating, we found a tiny kitten was trapped in the grill area of a big truck. Dave made the owner open the hood and undo the engine cap to free the kitten. Then we took him home and named him Jimmi, after the car in which he'd been found. Jimmi has been an amazing diversion and a warm, loving, sweet thing to comfort me when I'm down and depressed. We rescued him, and he rescued me right back.

Start tracking the God moments in your life. This way, you can look back and thank God for his generosity and mercy.

Date	God's Hand At Work in Your Life
Dec '07	Offer to buy business
June '08	Jimmi the kitten needed a rescue
July '08	Property sold

Psalms 46:1
God is our refuge and strength,
an ever-present help in trouble.

Chapter Ten Worksheet: Take Action . . . Now

What was the most powerful thought or strongest concept in this chapter for you?

_____
_____
_____
_____

If you implement one idea from this chapter, what would it be?

_____
_____
_____
_____

What do you plan to do differently as a result of what you read?

_____
_____
_____
_____

Which concept(s) would you like to share with family or friends?

_____
_____
_____
_____

Allow God's love to get you moving and grooving – NOW!

11. Stress Less over the Long Haul

2 Chronicles 5:13
He is good, his love endures forever.

The road may seem long, but God is with you every step of the way.

Hands-On Help

Finding time to take care of your loved one may be very difficult. You may be required to help him or her with daily activities such as getting dressed, bathing, feeding, and more. It's okay to feel stressed about this. Honesty is key. Ask your loved on for a little help. Even something as little as holding up his or her arms so you can get the coat on easier can go a long way. Another tip is to communicate openly. Tell him or her the plan. For example, I would tell Dad, "As soon as you finish taking your blood-sugar results, we'll go out to Annie's for dinner."

You must know your physical limits. If you cannot support your loved one or pick him or her up, please do not try. Both of you can end up injured, and this will cause unneeded stress. When my father started putting on weight, I could no longer take him out by myself. I simply couldn't manage getting him in and out of the car from his wheelchair. Luckily, for most of my father's illness, David was able to help. When David became too ill as well, I enlisted friends to assist. Sadly, though, we ended up going out less often since both Dad and Dave were seriously ill. I spent more time just visiting Dad at the nursing home than taking him out.

When David became wheelchair-bound later the same year, our sons and Dave's brother were on hand to assist most of the time. I learned techniques from the hospice nurses about how to move him without hurting him or my back.

Talk to Your Doctor

When you are under stress, any chronic or physical condition(s) you have may worsen. So make an appointment with your doctor and share that you have a new major life stressor. They will discuss how this might impact any chronic health condition(s) you have. You may want to explore antidepressants, depending on how you handle stress, the natural depression that comes with a chronically or terminally ill loved one, and facing significant life changes. Consider the following two statements:

> "About 60 percent of caregivers show signs of clinical depression, and caregivers take more prescription medications, including those for anxiety and depression, than others in their age group. Reluctance in asking for and accepting help is a major barrier to getting necessary respite and support."[1]

> "Major depressive disorder is a common psychiatric condition in the U.S. population. Symptoms of depression include general emotional dejection, withdrawal and restlessness that interfere with daily functioning, such as loss of interest in usual activities; significant change in weight, appetite, or both; insomnia; increased fatigue; feelings of guilt or worthlessness; slowed thinking or impaired concentration and suicide attempts or suicidal ideation."[2]

Do not consider yourself weak if you need some medical assistance coping. Some depression stems from a chemical imbalance, so it stands to reason that medication can assist you in dealing with depression.[3] While it may be unreasonable to expect medication to eliminate *all* the sadness or depression you feel. You can expect to feel more in control, though, of your emotions.

Depression and grief are natural parts of this process, and they cannot be medicated away. It can be tempting to think an extra drink at night or an extra pill will make everything better. The situation won't change, and you'll just have a headache to deal with the next day.

Additionally, there are significant dangers in becoming dependent on either antidepressants or alcohol to dull the pain of being a caregiver and/or of potentially losing your loved one. Alcoholism or drug addiction only starts you on a downward cycle that can result in losing your self-respect, your family's respect and support, your job, your home, and your health. Don't go there.

> *1 Peter 5:6–7*
> *Humble yourselves, therefore, under God's mighty hand, that he may lift you up in due time. Cast all your anxiety on him because he cares for you.*

Easier ER Visits

Make an ER kit you can grab and take with you just in case your loved one needs to go to the ER. Some of these items are necessary for your loved one, and some of them are for you. Either way, they will really come in handy. Include:

- A list of all the medications your loved one is taking. If you don't have a list, just round up all the pill bottles and put them in a plastic baggie to take along.
- Contact information for your children and close friends
- Your insurance cards
- A small book and pen to take notes
- A sweater or jacket (they keep ERs cold)
- Change for vending machines

- A good book, your Bible, or Bible study materials to help pass the time
- Puzzle books, needlework, or other portable hobbies

Pack a bag and keep it handy if you realize you are going to be making frequent ER or doctor visits where you will be doing lots of waiting.

Do not be afraid to ask a friend to drop you off and pick you up. After all, you may not be steady enough to drive yourself. You can even ask your friend to come along, just to keep you company. ER visits are very tedious and highly stressful. A buddy can help pass the time and reduce your stress level immensely.

Hebrews 13:6
So we say with confidence, the Lord is my helper;
I will not be afraid. What can man do to me?

Hospice Is Heaven-Sent

If your loved one becomes bedridden or too much for you to handle, consider hospice care. It will be easier to have more than just yourself as a caregiver.[3] The term hospice refers to an approach to end-of-life care as well as a type of facility for supportive care of terminally ill patients.

Hospice programs provide palliative, patient-centered care and other services. "Palliative" means the care relieves discomfort but does not improve the patient's condition or cure the disease. The goal of hospice care, whether delivered at home or a health-care facility, is the provision of humane and compassionate medical, emotional, and spiritual care to the dying.

The people who run hospice are angels on Earth, and they can help more than you'll ever be able to imagine. Depending on your loved one's age and insurance coverage, hospice care may be free to you, as Medicare with your insurance may cover costs.[2]

We were blessed that our insurance covered both my mother's and Dave's hospice care. We moved my mother to Midland Hospice for her last two weeks. It was a true blessing for her as she spent those two weeks pain-free. We chose to move Dave to Chicago for his last three weeks, having hospice care in our eldest son's home. This way, Dave could have easy access to both our sons and all six grandchildren—a gift to us all. We kept Dave in the home until the end, and it was a good decision for our family, but it may not right for everyone. Hospice will be able to help you understand and make those difficult decisions that await you.

Romans 8:28
And we know that in all things God works for the good of those who love him, who have been called according to His purpose.

Chapter Eleven Worksheet:
Stress Less over the Long Haul

What was the most powerful thought or strongest concept in this chapter for you?

_____

_____

_____

_____

If you implement one idea from this chapter, what would it be?

_____

_____

_____

_____

What do you plan to do differently as a result of what you read?

_____

_____

_____

_____

Which concept(s) would you like to share with family or friends?

_____

_____

_____

_____

*Allow God's love to sustain you and
give you strength.*

12. The Business of Death

You are never ready.

The Ultimate in Bad News

Discovering your loved one is not going to recover creates a major emotional setback. You will need time to process this information, and so will your loved one. Realize that, depending on his or her physical awareness or psychological situation at the time, the news may not actually sink in. My mother understood from the start that we were discussing the end; she was even able to help with her funeral arrangements. Dave, unfortunately, had significantly more challenges processing the information. The suddenness of the news and the level of chemical imbalances he was experiencing due to the illness made understanding difficult. It makes it doubly challenging when you have a disconnect between how the two of you are processing what the doctor is telling you. I would often have to call the doctor back to have him clarify, because Dave would be so adamant he heard the doctor say something different than what I heard.

After the initial shock of the diagnosis wears off, you need to get things in order. You need to be sure you know where everything is. It is better to do this early than wait for the disease to run its course; you never know if you will have a week, a month, or several more years to get all this done. Organizing all this information early will make you less stressed; there will be less to keep you from a good night's sleep.

Doctor Diligence

While prayer and faith are crucial, it is also important to remember to keep focused on the reality of the situation and symptoms. Be clear with your doctor, and tell him or her to communicate honestly with you. Learn as much as you can about the illness. If your loved one often forgets to tell his or her doctor about important information, tell the doctor yourself. Nobody knows your loved one like you, so it's important to maintain an open relationship with your doctor and nursing staff.[1]

Will-full Preparation

If you do not have a will, now is the time to draft one with your loved one. Stop and consider if you can handle being the executor of the estate or if you want someone else in that role.

For my mother, father, and aunt, I served as the executor. However, Dave and I appointed one of our sons as the executor of his will. I assumed it would not be in my best interest to play that part, nor did I think I would be in the mood to make so many decisions. It seemed appropriate to have assistance, and it proved a godsend. To avoid conflict between your children or step-children over the will, consider appointing an attorney or neutral third party as your executor.

Another tip: always consult with an attorney. Laws vary in each state, so find a lawyer who is knowledgeable about assets management.[2]

Get Power of Attorney

While you may not want to contemplate it, cancer or other illnesses may adversely impact your loved one's ability to think clearly.[3] Metastasis to the brain can have a devastating impact.[4] Even the long-term effects of chemotherapy can wear down one's faculties; it's called "chemo brain," when the patient can find it difficult to track and process new ideas and information.[5] Many terminal illnesses—like diabetes, Parkinson's, and Alzheimer's—also have a severe mental impact. Consult your doctor and consider getting medical power of attorney; if your loved one handled your household finances, you may need to take that over as well and need a financial power of attorney as well as a medical power of attorney for making final medical decisions.

Tough Talks

Discuss openly the options for using extended life support. You do not want to have to make end-of-life decisions without having had that discussion. Everyone in the immediate family needs to know the patient's wishes; that way, there are no hard feelings when one family member is not ready to let go while others are trying to honor the person's final choices. Also discuss funeral plans. Make this as lighthearted as possible, and consider having everyone plan at the same time. You want to know how the person wants the funeral and if he or she has any special wishes for it. We had that conversation with my mother, and it was very helpful in planning her service. She even told me exactly what she wanted sung. I have my own funeral planned and saved on my computer, so no one has to wonder what I will want. These days, funeral homes and churches are more open to personalizing the ceremony, so you should not be afraid to ask for something unusual if you know it would be appropriate for your loved one. Dad often joked about wanting to be buried upright with his golf clubs over his shoulder. He decided, however, he wanted to be cremated and have his ashes, along with Mom's, scattered in the ocean.

Prepaid and Planned = Prepared

I planned and prepaid for my father's funeral after being unprepared for my mother's death. I made the arrangements with the funeral home, prepaid for the cremation, and wrote the obituary. At the time of his death, I only had to make simple updates to his obituary, and I was done. Rather than having to make numerous decisions at a time full of grief, it was a very simple and a much easier process. Consider doing this for your peace of mind. It will significantly reduce your stress level at the time your loved one actually passes away.

Get Financial Information Together

Get all the information organized that you will need after your loved one's death: insurance policies, 401(k) or 403(b) statements, bank accounts, credit cards, IRAs, and other financial information. You may want to start consolidating retirement accounts early. This will help you avoid having to make too many financial decisions all at one time; plus, you'll be able to get your loved one's input into the decisions.

If you don't currently do the banking for the family, learn what needs to be done, what bills you have, how things are organized, what is set up on automatic deduction, and more. Get bills set up for automatic payment. Get car titles, stocks, and bonds signed over to you to avoid hassles and probate after your loved one passes.

If you do not have a credit card in your name, get one while your loved one is still alive. If you are one of many wives who has not worked in a while, and you are not working now, you may find it problematic getting credit after your spouse passes.

Work to Avoid Identity Theft

Identity theft of the deceased is increasingly common. Some tips to help avoid it are:

- Do not put all the identifying data in the obituary. For example, you needn't include the date of birth, city of birth, or the names of parents. These details make it easier for people to request copies of birth certificates to use in identity theft.
- Shred papers containing personal information.
- Use a product like ShredXP (ShredXP.com) to make sure data on hard drives is completely destroyed before giving computers away.
- Consider mailing bills at the post office or work instead of from your mailbox.
- Less is more when it comes to having personal information on your checks.
- Secure your PIN numbers, account numbers, and other sensitive information.
- Be sure your computer is secured with passwords more sophisticated than the word "password" or your pet's name.

Consider using ID security software such as Splash ID (SplashData.com).
- Watch your credit card bills for odd charges or information.
- Get periodic copies of your credit rating reports. This can be checked once a year for free at www.AnnualCreditReport.com.

You may think it will not happen to you, but within two weeks of Dave's death, someone had opened an account in his name in South Carolina and started charging large landscaping equipment to it.

If identity theft does happen, call your bank, freeze your credit cards, and file a police report immediately. The authorities will give you steps to follow that will help you stop the process and work to clear up the problems caused. This will take considerable time. Be persistent and patient.

Honor Their Memory

Work to imagine your loved one moving to a better place where you will see him or her again. If you are unsure of his or her belief in God, the time to discuss that is upon you. I personally love the song "I Can Only Imagine," by Mercy Me. I imagine Dave is free of pain and enjoying his everlasting life in the presence of God and Jesus.

There are countless ways to memorialize your loved one. When my mother passed away, we collected funds instead of asking for flowers. With that money, we started a memorial garden at our church. It has now become the memorial garden for everyone interested in doing this. The church has a beautifully landscaped area for reflective meditation that can be seen from the chapel. For my father, we started writing his autobiography right after Mother passed away. It was a two-year project, but we got it published and sent out to relatives the year before he passed away. It served as a great memorial for him.

Some people establish scholarships at the person's alma mater. Then children or young adults can reap the benefits, and your loved one's legacy lives on. Most funeral homes will now do a CD, DVD, or video for you if you provide photos or video clips. On one TV program I watched, the grandchildren each created a memory box. They used things around the house that reminded each child of the person. When they were finished, each child, regardless of age, had a unique and personal memory box.

On her reality show, Denise Richards spoke of having teddy bears made of her mother's clothes at *www.MemoryBearsByRobyn.com*. Our daughter-in-law made one using the shirt Dave wore in a photo taken with Wren, our newest grand-daughter, taken three days before he passed. Friends of ours lost their son suddenly when he was seventeen. They had many of his t-shirts made into memorial quilts. I've done this for our sons from Dave's t-shirts. Plus, I turned his ties into artwork for each son, and several pieces of art for myself.

> *Psalm 45:17*
> *I will perpetuate your memory through*
> *all generations; therefore the nations*
> *will praise you forever and ever.*

Fun Times Together

We often replay the bad events over and over. You need to find positive events to replay. Focus on the good events of your life and or marriage, and replay those instead. I've provided a few springboards if you don't know where to start or would like a little help.

- What was your favorite vacation?

  _____
  _____

- What will you remember most?

  _____
  _____

- What would you want people to know about your loved one's struggle?

  _____
  _____

- What have you learned from this illness?

  _____
  _____

- How do you want him or her to be remembered?

  _____

  _____

- What was the funniest thing you ever saw or experienced?

  _____

  _____

- What are you most glad you did?

  _____

  _____

- What are you most thankful for?

  _____

  _____

- What do you want those you leave behind to know?

  _____

  _____

Chapter Twelve Worksheet:
The Business Side of Death

What was the most powerful thought or strongest concept in this chapter for you?

_____

_____

_____

_____

If you implement one idea from this chapter, what would it be?

_____

_____

_____

_____

What do you plan to do differently as a result of what you read?

_____

_____

_____

_____

Which concept(s) would you like to share with family or friends?

_____

_____

_____

_____

Allow God's love to guide you in making sound decisions and give you peace.

13. Starting Over

Jeremiah 29:11
I know the plans I have for you, declares the Lord, plans to prosper
you and not to harm you, plans to give you hope and a future.

Become the person you are meant to be.

A New Beginning

Peter Peterson said, "Death is the only sure thing in life. Once we accept our own mortality and lose the fears of death, we can truly live a more fulfilling life."

You've also heard the concept that God works in mysterious ways. My neighbor has a wall hanging that reads, "When God leads you to the edge of the cliff, trust Him fully and let go. Only one of two things will happen. Either He will catch you when you fall, or He will teach you how to fly!" While I don't think this is exactly true, the power in that one sentence is amazing. God can shift things around for you today and let them work in your favor. God closes doors no man can open, and God opens doors no man can close.

Psalm 4:1
Answer me when I call to you, O my righteous
God. Give me relief from my distress;
be merciful to me and hear my prayer.

In working through Dave's imminent departure from this world, I started exploring what I wanted to do with my life after he was gone. The process really challenges you. Dave was not just my husband, but my business partner as well. He was my behind-the-scenes partner before he joined me full-time at the consulting business nine years later. Many of our friends and clients also said he was the other half of my brain. Sadly, it was definitely the better half—the logical and analytical half.

You have to realize the past will be dead, and the future you once imagined together is also gone. What you have now is the opportunity to imagine a new future. Who do you want to be?

Matthew 16:25
With God all things are possible.
For whoever wants to save his life will lose it,
but whoever loses his life for me will find it

What are the things you've always wanted to try?

_____
_____
_____
_____

What are things you did not do because you knew your loved one would not enjoy them?

_____
_____
_____
_____

What do you hear God whispering in your ear for you to focus on?

_____
_____
_____
_____

Psalm 142:2-3
I pour out my complaint before him; before him
I tell my trouble. When my spirit grows faint
within me, it is you who know my way. In the
path where I walk men have hidden a snare for me.

Have a blessed day, and remember to be a blessing to everyone you meet.

Mahatma Gandhi, the Indian philosopher esteemed for his doctrine of nonviolent protest, said, "Be the change you want to see in the world."

It is often darkest before the dawn. But with the dawn of each new day comes hope. There is hope that this day you will cry less. There is hope that you will thank God more for the gifts he gave you, the time you had together, and the opportunity to make a positive difference in someone else's life.

The sunrise is God's promise to you of new day and His love for you;
renew your promise to God to be your best self and share His love
with others.

For more information, to schedule seminars or to contact Cynthia B. Stotlar directly, go to: www.spiritual-support.org

May you be blessed in all you do! Cynthia

Chapter Thirteen Worksheet: Starting Over

What was the most powerful thought or strongest concept in this chapter for you?

_____

_____

_____

_____

If you implement one idea from this chapter, what would it be?

_____

_____

_____

_____

What do you plan to do differently as a result of what you read?

_____

_____

_____

_____

Which concept(s) would you like to share with family or friends?

_____

_____

_____

_____

Allow God's love to guide you as you walk this new path with Him at your side.

References

Throughout the entire book, the NIV Bible was used.

Copyright © 1973, 1978, 1984 by International Bible Society

Organizations:

American Cancer Society www.cancer.org
American Heart Association www.heart.org
American Institute of Stress www.stress.org
Family Caregivers Alliance www.caregiver.org
Food & Drug Administration www.fda.gov
National Family Caregivers Association www.nfcacares.org

Resource Books:

Adams, Mike. *Five Habits of Health Transformation.* Truth Publishing, LLC, 2006.

BibleGateway. New International Version, 2010. http://www.BibleGateway.com.

Blackaby, Henry and Richard Blackaby. *Hearing God's Voice.* Tennessee: B&H Publishing Group, 2002.

Byrne, Rhonda. *The Secret.* Simon & Schuster Adult, 2006.

Chan, Francis. *Crazy Love: Overwhelmed by a Relentless God.* David C. Cook, 2008.

Cordeiro, Wayne. *Attitudes that Attract Success.* Gospel Light, 2001.

Jenson, Mary. *Still Life: The Art of Nurturing a Tranquil Soul.* Oregon: Multnomah Publishers, Inc., 1997.

Levy, Lois. *Undress Your Stress.* Sourcebooks, Incorporated, 2005.

Lucado, Max. *Cure for the Common Life:
Living in Your Sweet Spot.* Tennessee: W Publishing Group, 2005.

Marshall III, Joseph. *Keep Going: The Art of Perseverance.*
Australia: Sterling Publishing Co., 2006.

Mercer, Michael and Maryann Troiani. *Spontaneous Optimism:
Proven Strategies for Health, Prosperity and Happiness.* Castlegate
Publishers, Incorporated, 1998.

Ryan, M.J. *Attitudes of Gratitude.* New York, New York:
MJF Books, 1999.

Schluter, Bonnie. *Love Letters from God:
Affirmations for Your Soul.* Oklahoma: Honor Books, 2000.

Wolpe, David. *Why Faith Matters.* New York, New York:
HaperCollins, 2008.

Endnotes

Chapter 1

1. Brown, Alane, "The Power of Meditation and Prayer," ArticleClick.com, http://www.articleclick.com/Article/ The-Power-of-Meditation-and-Prayer/1051320 (accessed 2010)

2. "The ACTS Pattern," prayerguide.org, http://www.prayerguide.org.uk/actsmodel.htm (accessed 2010)

3. Scott M.S, Elizabth "The Benefits of Forgiveness," stress. about.com, http://stress.about.com/od/relationships/a/ forgiveness.htm (accessed 2010) and

4. Fillon, Mike, "Holding a Grudge Can Be Bad for Your Health," webmd.com, http://webmd.com/news/20000225/ holding-a-grudge-can-be-bad-for-your-health (accessed 2010)

Chapter 2

1. "Treatment Programs at the Yale Depression Research Program," med.yale.edu, http://www.med.yale.edu/psych/ clinics/depression/study1.html (accessed 2010)

2. Mozumder, Sanjib, "Top 10 Simple Ways to Stay Fit," healthmad.com, http://healthmad.com/fitness/top-10- simple-ways-to-stay-fit/ (accessed 2010)

3. "Heart Disease and Caregiver Burnout," webmd.com, http://www.webmd.com/heart-disease/guide/heart- disease-recognizing-caregiver-burnout (accessed 2010)

4. Mozumder, Sanjib, "Top 10 Simple Ways to Stay Fit," healthmad.com, http://healthmad.com/fitness/top-10-simple-ways-to-stay-fit/ (accessed 2010)

5. AgingCare Staff, "Get More Energy by Eating Smart!," agingcare.com, http://www.agingcare.com/Articles/caregiver-exhaustion-fatigue-low-energy-139920.htm (accessed 2010)

6. Strausfogel, Sherrie, "Bathing Beauty" Copyright of Better Nutrition is the property of Active Interest Media, Inc.

7. "Stress Reduction, Stress Relievers," stress.org, http://www.stress.org/topic-reduction.htm (accessed 2010)

8. Whittle, Adrian, "Stress Relief - How Pets Can Reduce Your Stress Levels And Improve Your Health," ezinearticles.com, http://ezinearticles.com/?Stress-Relief--How-Pets-Can-Reduce-Your-Stress-Levels-And-Improve-Your-Health&id=502728 (accessed 2010)

9. Pepper, Leslie, "De-stress in 5 Minutes or Less!," parenting.com, http://www.parenting.com/article/de-stress-in-5-minutes-or-less-21355143 (accessed 2010)

10. Health.com editors, independent of sponsor, "Boost Your Mood With Color," healthe.com, http://living.health.com/2008/04/21/boost-your-mood-with-color/ (accessed 2010)

11. Bowling, MD, PhD, Allen C, "Musk and the Brain May be a Therapeutic Duet,"

12. "Cloud Watching," notsoboringlife.com, http://www.notsoboringlife.com/outdoor/cloud-watching/ (accessed 2010)

Chapter 3

1. National Family Caregivers Association, "Protect Your Health," thefamilycaregier.org, http://www.thefamilycaregiver.org/improving_caregiving/protect_your_health.cfm (accessed 2010)

2. National Family Caregivers Association, "Protect Your Health," thefamilycaregier.org, http://www.thefamilycaregiver.org/improving_caregiving/protect_your_health.cfm (accessed 2010)

3. Mozumder, Sanjib, "Top 10 Simple Ways to Stay Fit," healthmad.com, http://healthmad.com/fitness/top-10-simple-ways-to-stay-fit/ (accessed 2010)

4. "Relieving Stress with Exercise and Relaxation Techniques," stress-relief-exercises.com, http://www.stress-relief-exercises.com/index.html (accessed 2010)

5. "Deep Breathing Exercises Release Stress," stress-relief-exercises.com, http://www.stress-relief-exercises.com/deep-breathing-exercises.html (accessed 2010)

6. www.//GoodReads.com (accessed 2010)

Chapter 4

1. Kelly, Karen, "10 Foods that Love Your Heart," findarticles.com, http://findarticles.com/p/articles/mi_m0NAH/is_2_38/ai_n24220169/ (accessed 2010)

2. Ward, M.S., R.D., Elizabeth, "Breakfast Is Served, With a Side of Health Benefits," environmentalnutrition.com, http://www.environmentalnutrition.com/pub/30_10/features/151586-1.html (accessed 2010)

3. "Decreasing your Cancer Risk With Dark Chocolate," livestrong.com, http://www.livestrong.com/article/14876-decrease-your-cancer-risk-with-dark-chocolate/ (accessed 2010)

4. "5 Things You Need to Know About Antioxidants in Dark," livestrong.com, http://www.livestrong.com/article/4768-need-antioxidant-vitamins/ (accessed 2010)

5. "Eating Healthy on a Budget," livestrong.com, http://www.livestrong.com/article/67733-eating-budget/ (accessed 2010)

6. "Healthy Eating & Food Pyramids," livestrong.com. http://www.livestrong.com/article/394358-healthy-eating-the-food-pyramid/ (accessed 2010)

Chapter 5

1. "Laughter Moves Lymph and Oxygenates Your Organs," owygen-review.com, http://www.oxygen-review.com/laughter.html (accessed 2010)

2. "Laughter is the Best Medicine," helpguide.org, http://www.helpguide.org/life/humor_laughter_health.htm (accessed 2010)

3. Adams, Mike, "The Five Habits of Health Transformation," NaturalNews.com, http://www.naturalnews.com/011850.html (accessed 2010)

4. "Ray Bradbury Quotes," Thinkexist.com, http://thinkexist.com/quotes/ray_bradbury/ (accessed 2010)

5. Purcell, Maud LCSW, CEAP, "The Healing Power of Humor," Psychcentral.com, http://psychcentral.com/lib/2006/the-healing-power-of-humor/ (accessed 2010)

6. Clement, Doreene, "Journal Your Stress Away," Vidaville.com, http://www.vidaville.com/html/Journal-Your-Stress-Away-p-16436.html (accessed 2010)

7. "About Mattie Stepanek," Mattieonline.com, http://www.mattieonline.com/T_aboutMattie.htm (accessed 2010)

8. "Talking About Y0ur Problems Can Help," Betterhealth.vic.gov, http://www.betterhealth.vic.gov.au/BHCV2/bhcarticles.nsf/pages/Talking_about_your_problems_can_help?OpenDocument (accessed 2010)

9. Parachin, Victor, "Fears about Tears? Why Crying is Good for You," findarticles.com http://findarticles.com/p/search/?qt=fears+about+tears%3F+why+crying+is+good+for+you (accessed 2010)

10. Parachin, Victor, "Fears about Tears? Why Crying is Good for You," findarticles.com http://findarticles.com/p/search/?qt=fears+about+tears%3F+why+crying+is+good+for+you (accessed 2010)

11. "Song Therapy," Songtherapy.com, http://www.songtherapy.com/ (accessed 2010)

Chapter 6

1. "End-of-Life-Concerns," Childrensmercy.org, www.childrensmercy.org/Content/uploadedFiles/End%20of%20life.pdf (accessed 2010)

2. "A Wise Investment: Benefits of Families Spending Time Together," Familyfacts.org, http://www.familyfacts.org/briefs/15/a-wise-investment-benefits-from-families-spending-time-together (accessed 2010)

3. "Hibbies as Stress Relief," Ezinearticles.com, http://ezinearticles.com/?Hobbies-As-Stress-Relief&id=486452 (accessed 2010)

4. Reinberg, Steven, "Lack of Vitamin D Boost Death Risk," www.health.com, http://www.health.com/health/article/0,20411369,00.html (accessed 2010)

5. "How to Treat Yourself Right," Articlesbase.com, http://www.articlesbase.com/self-help-articles/how-to-treat-yourself-right-751877.html (accessed 2010)

Chapter 7

1. Schubiner, Howard, MD, "Ways to Heal Yourself Without Medicine," Keytostressfreeliving.com, http://www.keytostressfreeliving.com/ways-to-heal-yourself-without-medicine/ (accessed 2011)

2. Lobell, Leslie Karen, M.A., "Cultivating and Attitude of Gratitude … Even on a Bad Day," Enotalone.com, http://www.enotalone.com/article/1082.html (accessed 2010)

3. Williams, Erin, "DE-STRESS Your To-Do List," Erinwilliamscoaching.typepad.com, http://erinwilliamscoaching.typepad.com/erin_williams_coaching_bl/2011/03/weekly-directive-de-stress-your-to-do-list.html (accessed 2011)

Chapter 8

1. Reh, F. John, "Pareto's Principle—The 80-20 Rule," About.com, http://management.about.com/cs/generalmanagement/a/Pareto081202.htm (accessed 2010)

2. Ewer, Cynthia, "Free Printables For Garage or Yard Sales," Organizedhome.com, http://organizedhome.com/time-money/garage-sale-savvy-free-printables (accessed 2010)

3. Bell, Kay, "Tax valuation guide for donated goods," Bankrate.com, http://www.bankrate.com/finance/money-guides/tax-valuation-guide-for-donated-goods.aspx (accessed 2010)

4. Gorgan, Elena, "Organization as the Key to a Stress-Free Life," Softpedia.com, http://news.softpedia.com/news/Organization-as-the-Key-to-a-Stress-Free-Life-96037.shtml (accessed 2010)

5. Crawshaw, Caitlin, "Dare to Divvy Up Your Duties at Work," Edmontonjournal.com, http://www.thetelegram.com/Business/Employment/2010-01-11/article-1436854/Dare-to-divvy-up-your-duties-at-work/1 (accessed 2010)

6. Family Caregiver Alliance, "Hiring In-Home Help," Caregiver.org, http://www.caregiver.org/caregiver/jsp/content_node.jsp?nodeid=407 (accessed 2010)

7. Rodgers, Gail, "Bringing Balance to Your Life," Powertochange.com, http://powertochange.com/life/balancelife/ (accessed 2011)

8. Family Caregiver Alliance, "Taking Care of YOU: Self-Care for Family Caregivers," Caregiver.org, http://www.

caregiver.org/caregiver/jsp/content_node.jsp?nodeid=847 (accessed 2011)

9. Medvescek, Christina, "Caregivers Say "Yes" to Offers of Help," Alsm.mda.org, http://alsn.mda.org/article/caregivers-say-yes-offers-help (accessed 2010)

Chapter 9

1. Piper, John, "A Passion for the Supremacy of God for the Joy of All Peoples,' Desiringgod.org, http://www.desiringgod.org/resource-library/sermons/a-passion-for-the-supremacy-of-god-for-the-joy-of-all-peoples (accessed 2010)

2. "Volunteer," Networkforgood.org, http://www1.networkforgood.org/for-donors/volunteer (accessed 2010)

Chapter 11

1. Family Caregiver Alliance, "Taking Care of YOU: Self-Care for Family Caregivers," Caregiver.org, http://www.caregiver.org/caregiver/jsp/content_node.jsp?nodeid=847 (accessed 2011)

2. "FDA Approves Emsam (Selegiline) as First Drug Patch for Depression," Fda.gov, http://www.fda.gov/NewsEvents/Newsroom/PressAnnouncements/2006/ucm108607.htm (accessed 2010)

3. Family Caregiver Alliance, "Taking Care of YOU: Self-Care for Family Caregivers," Caregiver.org, http://www.caregiver.org/caregiver/jsp/content_node.jsp?nodeid=847 (accessed 2011)

4. "Medicare Hospice Benefits," Medicare.gov, www.medicare.gov/publications/pubs/pdf/02154.pdf (accessed 2011)

Chapter 12

1. Family Caregiver Alliance, "Communicating With Your Dictor, Part I," Caregiver.org, http://www.caregiver.org/caregiver/jsp/home.jsp (accessed 2010)

2. Family Caregiver Alliance, "Durable Powers of Attorney and Revocable Living Trusts," Caregiver.org, http://www.caregiver.org/caregiver/jsp/content_node.jsp?nodeid=434 (accessed 2010)

3. Goldberg, Stan, "Understanding chronic and terminal illnesses: A guide for healthy people," Examiner.com, http://www.examiner.com/end-of-life-issues-in-san-francisco/understanding-chronic-and-terminal-illnesses-a-guide-for-healthy-people (accessed 2010)

4. National Cancer Institute, "Dictionary of Cancer Terms," Cancer.gov, http://www.cancer.gov/dictionary (accessed 2010)

5. The American Cancer Society, "Chemo Brain," Cancer.org, http://www.cancer.org/treatment/treatmentsandsideeffects/physicalsideeffects/chemotherapyeffects/chemo-brain (accessed 2010)

Look upward to God to see the richness of life...He has plans for you!

CPSIA information can be obtained at www.ICGtesting.com
Printed in the USA
LVOW060749240312

274539LV00003B/2/P